THUNDERCLAP

A Defining Silence

Juliane Corn Lee

To Sara

Best —

Juliane.

PISCES
PRESS
SAN FRANCISCO

Published by Pisces Press
236 West Portal Avenue, #551
San Francisco, California

Permissions acknowledgments appear on page 215.

Printed in the United States of America
First Edition: December 2018

10 9 8 7 6 5 4 3 2 1

Lee, Juliane Corn
Thunderclap: A Defining Silence

ISBN (paperback): 978-0-692-14242-4
ISBN (ebook): 978-0-578-40261-1

Library of Congress Control Number: 2018954141

Cover photograph and cover design by Eugene Lee.
Interior layout by Andrew Benzie, www.andrewbenziebooks.com
Author photo by James Brian Studios, www.jamesbrian.com

To Steven

CONTENTS

ACKNOWLEDGMENTS

This book would not have been possible without the loving and steady support of my brother, Eugene Lee. His contributions over the years have been far-reaching and nothing short of extraordinary, from his guidance early on in developing the book's structure, to reading drafts, and finally to the arresting book cover design. Eugene has confirmed once and for all that his creative genius extends beyond the canvas.

I would like to acknowledge my editor, Signe Jorgenson, who gently guided and challenged me to write outside my comfort zone, to "show" rather than "tell" my story. Her vision has made this a stronger book.

To my "angels," friends that served as advisers and proofreaders: Rose Dito, Jan Jue, Ruth Sleeper, Rose Pinard, Stephanie Solar, Cameron Ostovar, Dee Williams, and Lizl Pienaar.

Special mention must also be given to the naysayers. Their words kept me focused and strengthened my resolve to complete this book.

To my parents, siblings, and extended family: Thank you for enriching my life, as reflected within these pages.

PROLOGUE

San Francisco Bay Area, March 1988

"This is a time of sudden catastrophic events," began my *I Ching* fortune.

An event of catastrophic proportions was unknown to me. My life to that point had been relatively easy—requiring little reflection—and the price one can pay for such circumstances is a life that is lived on the surface: the perfect look and, by all accounts, the perfect life, I suppose.

Several weeks after my twenty-sixth birthday, I was at home with my siblings Eugene and Genny; bored, we decided to do the *I Ching*, which is a 2,000-year-old system of fortunetelling from China. From the vast interpretations of this ancient oracle in contemporary terms, the book we had found most useful was by Sam Reifler. His book *I Ching: A New Interpretation for Modern Times* provides a comprehensive translation of the original texts.

Having been introduced to the oracle only a few years before, the readings had immediately appealed to our metaphysical sides—a way, perhaps, of receiving messages from the Universe. Yet we practiced it more as a diversion by occasionally consulting it and applying its answers to our questions when it felt right, thus relying more on intuition than anything else.

Although the *I Ching* can be consulted alone, we developed our own method of consulting it as a group. So, we sat in a circle on the living room floor that evening and decided that I should have the first turn. Initially, I didn't have a particular question in mind. I had gotten engaged to my boyfriend only a few months before, which diminished my uncertainties regarding our four-year relationship. With our wedding set for September, it was as if everything in my life was, in fact, a certainty. And so it came to be that on this particular evening, I was at a complete loss for a question.

After several minutes, I decided on a whim to ask if San Francisco's Big Earthquake would happen that year as many had predicted. Since the infamous earthquake in 1906, it has been said that an even stronger one, the Big One, would inevitably occur and result in the city's total destruction. It seemed as if different groups foretold it was "the year" for the dreaded event almost annually. I frequently came across such talk in newspaper or magazine articles that featured either some ancient prophecy or recognized and unknown psychics of the day. That year, it was rumored—within my circle of friends, at least—the fateful time had arrived.

Having decided on a question, my consultation began. I closed my eyes, shook three coins between my cupped hands, and concentrated on my question. Over and over, it went through my mind: *Will the Big Earthquake happen this year?* Once I felt I had concentrated enough, I tossed the coins onto the floor. On this occasion, Genny was tasked with reading aloud the outcome of the tosses.

"Okay, you have two tails and one head," she said.

She then proceeded to write on a piece of paper the symbol that represents this specific combination of heads and tails, one straight line: _____. Another toss would later prompt Genny to write a broken line, ___ ___, which represents the corresponding combination of one tail and two heads. This process of asking a question and tossing the coins is repeated a total of six times; after each toss, a new line is written vertically and stacked on top of the previous line. The first toss result is on the bottom, and each one that follows is above it. The symbol created at the end of the process refers to a particular reading, known as a "hexagram."

Besides making the *I Ching* a group experience, our method included having a designated individual read the resulting hexagram out loud. One of the advantages of this group consultation was that we could then share our interpretations of the readings so that the questioner could arrive at a conclusion that felt right.

Each hexagram in the *I Ching* is interpreted in three different ways. First, there is a general reading that represents an overview of one's life (Artha). Another addresses relationships (Kama), and the final reading speaks to one's spiritual life (Moksha). The following were the six lines that I received that night:

As always, I shared my question with the others only after obtaining the hexagram. "My question is, 'Will the Big Earthquake happen this year?'" Referring to a table in the book, Eugene then took over from Genny and quickly looked up my specific hexagram. I then received my "answer," reading number 51, entitled, "The Thunderclap." Eugene began to read:

One's life (Artha):

This is a time of sudden catastrophic events. Remain cool. Expect a general reaction of shock and fear and then hysteria. Do not get caught up in it. If you retain a deep acceptance of the inevitability of the present moment, then you will ride out the present widespread catastrophe wiser and stronger than you were before.

Relationships (Kama):

You and Friend have been struck by an unforeseen and seemingly disastrous event. If you react with selfish anxieties you will start blaming each other for whatever has occurred. If you hysterically fantasize yourselves out of seeing the reality of the catastrophe, it will overcome you. If you remain calm and meet your problems in the same warm and loving spirit with which, up till now, you have met your pleasures, then this disaster can only benefit you in the long run by deepening the bond between you.

Spiritual life (Moksha):

A time of catastrophic "acts of God" is a good time to examine the depth of your spiritual commitment. With an enlightened point of view you have learned to accept the bad moments of your life. You have learned not to grasp possessively at the good moments. You have lived in a state of peace and equanimity. But in the face of the present disasters you are rediscovering fears and anxieties in yourself. Thus you do *not* completely, deeply, effortlessly accept the will of God. You have not thrown off your ego so thoroughly that you can face these times with a Buddhalike calm. It is good that you have discovered this. It points to where you must now strive on your path to complete enlightenment.

"Huh? What? What does that mean?" Genny, Eugene, and I asked one another. At the time, I could relate it neither to my question about the earthquake nor to my life in general. All this aside, what did it mean by "catastrophic events"? My sense from the reading was that this catastrophe was not characteristic of an earthquake but rather more of an individual experience, suggesting that it could impact my relationship with my fiancé. But with our wedding only six months away, I was certain that our loving and committed relationship would only continue to grow. In short, how could this hexagram be true when I was at a good point in my life?

After a while, when we still could not make sense of it, we simply decided it was a bad reading and moved on to the next person. As I'd later discover, the truth of this hexagram would be apparent in retrospect. I would later come to fully understand the meaning of the reading, and of the events that would radically alter the course of my life.

But please allow me to tell my story from the very beginning.

PART ONE

YOU HAVE LIVED IN A STATE OF
PEACE AND EQUANIMITY

CHAPTER ONE

The Early Years

"If this child you're carrying is a girl,"
proclaimed the psychic, "you must <u>not</u> give her a name with
a 'J.' Only then will you finally have boys."

After having four daughters in succession, my mother, who was a proud, independent woman pregnant with her fifth child, did not like to admit she was desperate for a boy. So, when she was told by a fortuneteller that the reason she only had girls was because each child's name began with the same letter, her response was immediate. She sat back with her arms crossed in front of her, the short strap of her handbag safely nestled in one arm. Then, using her thumb, she began to fiddle with the back side of the large diamond platinum ring on her finger. Perhaps my mother did her best to seem unfazed by what she had just heard, to not give any clue as to what she was actually thinking. As the youngest daughter of a strong and controlling man, she *was* used to accepting directives, if only from him. Ironically, though, it was partly because of her father—Papa, as we called him—that Mommy was not one to be told what she could or could not do. Yet in the end, when she gave birth later that year, she hewed to superstition even while maintaining some semblance of control. She decided to name her fifth child, our baby sister, Genny. Then, as foretold, Mommy would finally give birth to two sons in the years that followed: Eugene and Glenn.

Born and raised on the remote island of Guam in the West Pacific, our life in those early days can best be described as simple. My birth in 1962 was not significantly marked by the winds of change and "revolution" that defined America in the 1960s, which is perhaps what makes those early days all the more significant. Indeed, though Guam is a territory of the U.S., its remote location and traditional Asian-influenced values stood in sharp contrast to the changing face of its parent country. Lying west of the International Date Line, Guam is best known for being "Where America's Day Begins," a slogan often inscribed on souvenirs, and to me in those early days, this vague reference was about all I knew of the modern world and the people in it.

The small island provided the perfect setting for my privileged life away from the hustle and bustle of the times. In the capital of Agaña, for instance, landmarks were used instead of street signs when giving directions, and most of the island's two-lane streets were lined with a mix of coconut trees and electricity poles. It was easy to see that the island was somewhere between a budding metropolis and an ancient paradise.

In addition to this contrast with the typical notion of 1960s America, my own early years stand out as incredibly unique. From birth until age seven, I lived not in the stereotypical nuclear family household but in a large compound that housed my parents and six siblings as well as our extended family, headed by Papa.

My maternal grandfather, Charles Corn, a Chinese national, had immigrated to Guam soon after the Second World War. Because he was a well-respected and prominent businessman on the island and because my mother was completely devoted to him, our world revolved around my grandfather for as long as he lived. Our identities both as individuals and as a family were rooted in the fact that we were the wife, child, or grandchild of Charles Corn. He was a legend both in and outside of our home, a fact that was ingrained in us from the earliest years. Renowned as one of the wealthiest businessmen on the island, he was also known as a man who possessed great humility. Once, when Papa was pulled over for a traffic violation, the young officer took his license and immediately acknowledged him. "Oh, Mr. Corn," he nervously began. "I'm sorry, but you were driving over the speed limit, so I'll have to write you a ticket, Sir." Later, it was said that Papa dropped by the police station and asked for his good friend—the police captain—to commend the young officer for his diligent work.

Growing up, Mommy didn't read to us but instead told stories of Papa's life, impressing upon us all the importance of his role in our lives and the world at large.

Tales of his time with the resistance movement in Japanese-occupied China were among my favorites. She used these stories to teach us important life lessons as well as to keep us entertained and enamored. One example is the tale of the time when Papa was interrogated by the Japanese. He was asked by the commanding officer, "Which country do you love more—China or Japan?"

Without hesitation, Papa responded, "China, because it is my country, and if I were to answer differently you wouldn't believe me."

It was at this point that Papa was released from the prison camp while those that answered otherwise were executed. This sort of bravery in the face of total destruction, which some would falsely label as simply ego, defined his entire life, its successes and its faults. With those stories embedded within me at an early age by my mother's countless retellings, it's not surprising that Papa became a larger-than-life figure to me, like a hero in a Hollywood film.

The life he provided for us all rivaled the best films of the time. Our extended family lived in a Chinese-style home that was known throughout the island as "the Pagoda."

The majestic, white five-story structure with blue-and-red trim was nestled on a shrub-covered cliff overlooking Agaña Bay. True to its name, the Pagoda included a tower and had roofs that curved upward on each story. The half-mile road that led to the main entrance of our home was just off a main street and, like the city, the physical and social structure of our home embraced that same gray area between the worlds of old and new.

Papa was an early riser. Therefore, my older sisters and I would find him in the kitchen on most mornings once we began school. He stood by the dining table where he would line up the lunches he had personally prepared for us—ham or Spam sandwiches with mayonnaise and white bread, carefully wrapped in a napkin and aluminum foil.

Although we're not bilingual, the one Chinese phrase he had taught us to say was "good morning."

My sisters and I would always say "Jóusàhn, Papa" as we walked by to pick up our lunches.

Dressed in his customary casual attire, long, gray silk shorts down to his knees and a white tank top, he stood on the opposite side of the table. With a wide grin that revealed his full set of crooked, yellowed teeth, he'd respond in turn to each of us as we went by: "Ah, jóusàhn...jóusàhn, nuy-nuy!" He nodded his head in delight and said "Good morning, little girl" as though he had just heard us master the Chinese language.

While it's true that we lived in a traditional Chinese-style, multi-generational home, this was offset by the fact that it contained everything a modern family could need or want: air conditioners, washing machines and clothes dryers, and television sets in most rooms (albeit in black-and-white, since color sets were not readily available on the island).

Our front door led directly into an area with a sunken fountain at its center. Taking up most of the space, the square fountain had a large red pillar in each of its four corners and red benches along its sides. This structure's prominence in the middle of the Pagoda was part of what made it the very heart of our home, and it stands out in my memories of the place. I especially liked the sound it made whenever it rained. In a hot, tropical climate like Guam, the intense humidity only accelerated during these times, yet the sound of raindrops falling into the fountain from the screened skylight above provided a modicum of serenity despite the penetrating heat.

During the holidays, a large tree stood on a pedestal at the very center of the fountain. One Christmas Eve, when I was about five, we excitedly gathered as our gifts were handed out. While our teenage cousins sat in the nearby living room, the younger children gathered around the fountain, like we did each year. The Christmas carols that blared from the phonograph that night seemed to play in sync with the sound of wrapping paper being torn all around me.

As always, I sat beside my cousin Christine. Since we were close in age, we were playmates and often received the same gifts. That year was no exception. "It's Tina, Tina the Ballerina!" we cried. Within minutes, we practiced pushing the tiara on top of our dolls' heads to control their movement. Always en pointe, the twenty-four-inch doll could walk and even spin like a ballerina. Then, my attention turned to the commotion on the other side of the fountain.

"Look, look!" Eugene squealed with delight. We all ran towards Eugene and saw that Uncle had given him a baby chick. It had popped out of the box he'd just opened. "Look, look!" he said over and over as he tried to grab hold of the chick. A toddler still, Eugene's chubby legs wobbled as he tried to keep up with the chick that scurried about on the fountain bench. Mommy stood behind him, hunched over with her hand right by his back to ensure he didn't fall.

I then felt a tug on my dress. "My name's Johnny!" Genny announced. Then she fired her toy gun, which was pointed up at me. "Bang! Bang!" My baby sister stood there dressed in an outfit identical to mine: a kelly-green jumper dress and a yellow cotton blouse. She was obsessed with John Wayne films, and three-year-old Genny walked around the fountain that night donning a red cowboy hat and firing her gun in two rapid successions before placing it in the holster around her waist.

I later walked over to the side of the fountain where my older sisters sat with their treasured Barbie doll cases in tow. My eldest sister Jocelyn—whose family nickname is Che-Che— had just dressed her Barbie in the gift she'd received: a long, light blue satin cape with a white fur collar.

"Wow! It looks like a movie star's coat!" Jasmine exclaimed.

Che-Che had her hand wrapped around Barbie's ankles as she held the doll upright, and she turned her wrist to make the cape swing from side to side. My other two sisters—Joyce and Jasmine—then took their turns twirling Che-Che's Barbie. Mesmerized by the brilliant blue cape and reaching for the doll, I cried, "It's my turn, it's my turn. I wanna try!"

"No Julie, you might break it," Che-Che replied. "You know you're too young to play with Barbie. But here, you can touch it. But remember, be gentle."

I thought the cape was the most beautiful thing I'd ever

seen. I think I even held my breath as I ran my fingertips lightly from top to bottom, for the cape felt as luxurious and as cool to the touch as it looked.

A few feet away from that central point were the stairs that led to the infamous tower. Our over-protective mothers believed that the wooden stairway leading to the tower was dangerous simply because it was long, and as a result, the grandchildren were prohibited from setting foot in the area. They would remark, "Don't go up there. It's dark and scary." This sense of fear was so ingrained in me that I don't recall ever being curious to discover what was up those ominous stairs. Obediently, I would sit only on the first few steps of the forbidden staircase. Years later, our mothers created a barricade when they learned that some of the older boys had begun secretly exploring the restricted zone. I never participated in these expeditions myself and was appalled by my older cousins' disobedience. It was a bit of a letdown when I later learned the tower was just a small, circular room with windows on all sides that offered a panoramic view of the island and the vast blue Pacific Ocean.

The most notable of the Pagoda's features was not the most prominent physically, but it spoke most clearly about the man my grandfather had become. On the wall by the front door was a collection of black-and-white photographs depicting the highs of Papa's life. Many of them were autographed photos of the numerous acquaintances Papa had made during his stay in Manila in the 1930s, where he met his wife and had his children. His years there were the first stop on his journey to America. As a principal concessionaire in U.S. military bases, he developed strong ties with many high-ranking officials and was able to build his own fortune as a result. When I began school, the man that I came to know as General Douglas MacArthur

Papa and Mama in the 1950s, with the
Pagoda's tower looming in the backdrop.

My six siblings and I with Papa and Mama in our playroom at the Pagoda months before the birth of our baby brother, Glenn. In the foreground, from left, Jasmine, Joyce and me. Che-Che is seated behind me, followed by Eugene and Genny. May 1969.

became more than just one of the faces that stared down at me in my youth. Besides depicting his trademark sunglasses, broad smile, and Field Marshal's cap, the signed photo read, "To my friend Charlie Corn, Douglas MacArthur."

Another prominently displayed photograph was that of Dwight and Mamie Eisenhower. It was Eisenhower who had suggested to Papa—who was then known as Chan Yao Kuhn—that he adopt the western name of Charles Corn. His surname, Corn, is the middle name I bear to this day.

Indeed, the Pagoda was our fortress, and like a fortress, it nurtured and protected us during the years we lived there. It was a perfect haven from the unknown and, at times, frightening world outside. Although the Pagoda was a 24,000-square-foot home, we occupied only one floor, a common Chinese characteristic used to emphasize the group's importance rather than that of the individual.

More significant, perhaps, was that protected innocence and the group-mind characteristic defined the early years of my life and the way in which I would interpret the world for many years to come. As the granddaughter of Charles Corn, my life was not wholly my own, nor did any other member of my family truly have his or her own life. As such, we were docile children who did as we were told, and we never questioned the rules that were set in place. Furthermore, not having a claim to my own life taught me to completely rely on others for my care. It did not impress upon me a sense of self-reliance.

Not unlike a Hollywood character, Papa's life followed a careful arc of development ruled by his own directives. His wife (my grandmother, whom we affectionately called Mama) was a beautiful young *mestiza* girl with chestnut hair and hazel eyes. Mama was a perfect blend of her Filipina mother and English-American father. Hailing from a family of little means, her marriage to my grandfather was as much emblematic of his obsession with America as one borne of love. He made his preference for Chinese people over others clear to anyone who would listen and eventually took a second wife in Hong Kong—as he once put it, "a Chinese wife"—to reinforce that preference. But his obsession with America was also a dominant theme in his life and, ultimately, in my life. Mama just reinforced it.

Mama's role in the family was much different from her husband's. While Papa had been an overbearing figure throughout our lives, my grandmother was a calming presence amidst the storm of Papa's personality. Perhaps it was her cultural differences that set Mama apart, or perhaps it was the strain that resulted from years of Papa's relentless control.

Theirs was a relationship symbolic of the times, another example of the blend between the old and new. Although it was an arranged marriage (Mama was sixteen when a much older Charlie Corn contracted her for marriage), this did not prevent a constant struggle for control to dominate their union. Mama notoriously spent money, without regard to what Papa would approve of. This habit directly influenced his choice to take on a second wife, who was quite the opposite of my grandmother.

Although she was not as beautiful, Papa's "Chinese" wife was well-educated and possessed a knack for making money. Together, they created a sizable fortune in Hong Kong and Papa often extolled her business acumen, even in Mama's presence. Because of his regard for her, his Chinese wife's status was not as one beneath Mama; she was simply Mama's counterpart in his Hong Kong family. As a distinct yet venerated part of his life, his second family had Papa's original surname, Chan, and when family members referred to his other wife in conversation, they called her "Mama Chan."

CHAPTER TWO

The Pagoda

Papa cherished the Pagoda. To him, it symbolized all that he had accomplished as a child from humble beginnings in Guandong, China who became a highly-respected and successful American businessman. Throughout his life, he continually expanded or renovated parts of the house, firmly believing that it would somehow prolong his life. This idea was reflected throughout the structure of the Pagoda itself. Enclosing the simple wooden front porch were blue beams that supported large carved Chinese characters that said "Long Life" and were painted boldly in red. The characters were also found throughout the interior of the house, enclosed in rectangular wooden frames above the doorways of the main rooms.

Living at the Pagoda was unlike anything most Americans of my generation experienced, and, in many ways, it shaped my outlook on life and family for many years to come. As the head of the house and its rightful owners, Papa and Mama lived in the main section, while their children, along with their own families, occupied the rest of the space in and around the structure proper. As the favorite child, my mother, along with her husband (my father) and their children, lived in the part of the house that was closest to Papa. Auntie and her family lived in yet another portion of the main floor, and Uncle and his family lived in a small home within the family compound.

Despite the communal atmosphere of this arrangement, there was some separation. For example, Auntie's section of the main floor included a kitchen, dining room, and living room. However, the entire extended family frequently gathered for an informal dinner with Papa and Mama, uniting us as a group.

Though these gatherings were never planned, there always seemed to be enough room for those who showed up. It was easy to fit at least a dozen people around the red, circular dining table at the center of the main dining room. Then, if more seats were needed, the younger children would simply sit on an available adult's lap.

As in other situations, Papa was an imposing presence during these family dinners. The table's circular nature did not prevent him from sitting at its "head" to command attention and control the room by operating the motorized Lazy Susan that sat at the center of the table. Operated by a switch located directly underneath the table where Papa sat, the younger grandchildren always clamored to sit next to him because it meant having the honor of commanding the switch and therefore absorbing some of his power.

Papa dominated our life at the Pagoda, and in many ways, his presence and mood at any given time were a barometer for our actions and family dynamic. This was most apparent among his three children. There was a hierarchy among the siblings, and his power and control over his youngest child—my mother—was the most absolute. She did everything she could to please him, even ending a serious romance at Papa's behest simply because her young suitor was not Chinese. The worst-case scenario for her, I suspect, was to be the target of his criticism, which is what happened when anyone dared to defy him. She was therefore dutiful to a fault and did as she was told without question.

She consented to have Papa raise three of her seven children: Jasmine, Eugene, and Glenn. More than anything else, this decision illustrates my mother's loyalty and devotion to her father. She never openly discussed the matter, but I sensed her struggle to come to terms with this particular arrangement in the years that followed.

Although they lived with Papa and Mama in their section of the family home, it was Mommy who drove them to and from school or medical appointments, along with the rest of us.

It helped that Papa was equally fond of and devoted to my own father, whom we called Daddy. Papa's preference for Chinese suitors helped immensely in this regard. Daddy easily won Papa's approval with the added plus of being from the same province in China as Papa. In fact, only a mountain stands between their home villages. Papa couldn't have hoped for a more suitable son-in-law, and thus my parents' role in the family was elevated substantially even though my mother was both the youngest child and a girl.

His influence was different with us grandchildren, though. Papa enjoyed having us around him and consequently spent a great deal of time with us. He alone, unaccompanied by any other adult, would pack as many of us as he could into his car for a Sunday drive to his properties around the island. And, despite our numbers, Papa had a special way of making each of us feel acknowledged. A look into his eyes or a pat on my head was all it would take to make me feel like he and I were the only ones in the room. This was perhaps the quality that drew people from all walks of life to him and explained his associations with President Eisenhower and other dignitaries of his time. When he encountered acquaintances while we were out, he always introduced each one of us to them, taking the time to recognize the importance we played in his life. By sharing us with his acquaintances, he also acknowledged the role that they played in his life.

Considering his close relationship with my parents, it was no surprise that Papa was particularly fond of my siblings and me, a fact he never bothered to downplay. In addition to raising three of my mother's children himself, he treated our accomplishments as if they outweighed those of the other grandchildren; previously, my mother's achievements had outweighed those of her own siblings. For example, by the time my mother had given birth to her long-awaited first son, Eugene, Papa already had several grandsons by Auntie and Uncle. Yet in his joy and excitement, he planned a lavish celebration for Eugene's baptism as though he were the first-born boy. Eugene's party that year was the largest one ever held for any grandchild; a thousand guests were invited to the Pagoda.

Despite our honored role, even we were aware of Papa's dark side. If he told us to be quiet, we followed his instruction without hesitation. His temper was easily provoked, and we had all witnessed too many of his confrontations with Mama and the other adults to chance encountering it on our own. His wife and children were the principal recipients of his wrath. He would not hesitate to yell critical and disparaging words, leaving the objects of his rage cowering and silent.

CHAPTER THREE

Life on the Island

"Here, let's spin the globe and see who can find Guam first!" Che-Che said as she spun the small globe in her hand. My other two older sisters huddled close to her as I elbowed my way between them. I stood on tiptoe in my red-and-white rubber zoris, struggling to finally be the first one to find that particular part of blue—an expanse of water—where I knew Guam sat, alone, in isolation.

"There, there it is!" Joyce declared. Although I was never able to pinpoint it first, I'd learned to join them in shrieking with delight once it was spotted.

"Wow, look how its name is even larger than the island," Jasmine said as she pointed to the speck of green that represented our home.

Surely it sat alongside other specks, but I could only focus on how sharply it contrasted with the chunks of land in various colors above and below it. It's not surprising that later, when I learned Guam was merely a territory of America and not a bona fide state, I came to believe the mainland was better in every respect. They had better weather, better schools, and better stores. They had, in short, the best of everything.

I didn't realize it at the time, but we were as much of a mystery to others on the island as those large masses on our globe were to us. I came to understand this years later, while at a party during my college years in San Francisco. I met a woman there whose childhood home was near ours.

As though she didn't want anyone else in the room to hear her, she looked me in the eye and confessed, almost in a whisper, "You know, I have to say, the other neighborhood kids and I wondered if there were really children living at the Pagoda. In all those years, we had never seen any of you." I could only nod and smile in response. After all, how could I begin to explain the reason for it?

We were allowed to play outdoors only occasionally, and only for a few hours in the late afternoons. In addition to our mothers' eccentric notion that perspiring was a clear indication of physical overexertion, they preferred that we have lighter skin. The idea was (and still is among the Chinese) that attractiveness is measured by the fairness of your skin tone. This belief, which, no doubt stems from old-country thinking, only accentuated the line between old and new that we seemed to always straddle—one's complexion indicated one's social class, thus lighter skin was highly prized.

I remember the first time I was allowed to play outdoors with the toy I had received on my birthday that year. The battery-operated Thunderbird Roadster was beige and had red vinyl seats for two. My cousin Christine was, of course, seated beside me. We must have been around six years old. We had raided our mothers' closets, and we each donned a scarf tightly wrapped around our heads as we struggled to keep our large, dark sunglasses in place. Our parents' cars had been removed from the Pagoda's large, shady driveway, so we had ample space to drive around the area before heading out, with the other kids on their bikes, to the small road leading to Uncle's house.

Our cousin George—who had been complaining to his parents that he should also have a car like mine—was showing

Genny and Eugene drive my roadster in the Pagoda's living room.

off the new red, open two-seat car his dad had gotten him. Throughout our playtime that day, George's nanny was, as always, running closely behind him. Whenever she could convince him to take a break, she'd hastily wipe him down with a towel and then, as instructed by his mother, who supervised from afar, sprinkle him with baby powder to ensure he was dry and cool. Even though Auntie stood on the covered porch, she wore dark sunglasses and an unbuttoned long-sleeve cotton blouse over her dress to shield her arms from the setting sun's remaining rays.

Mommy and our other aunt stood at the edge of the driveway, supervising us all. "Slow down!" our mothers instructed the boys on their bicycles.

George then drove in front of us and yelled to Christine and me, "I'll show you guys! I'll beat you because my car is better and it's faster!"

"Oh, leave us alone, *Georgie Porgie!*" I yelled back, annoyed.

"Yeah, leave us alone, *Georgie Porgie,*" Christine bellowed, "because we're on our way to Town House to go shopping!" Christine and I laughed as we straightened our scarves and sunglasses, then took off to catch up with the older kids on their bikes. *Beep! Beep!* I honked the horn as we whirred past George.

At sunset, our mothers called out to us. "Okay, it's time to go back in for dinner. Come on! Let's go in now!"

"MMM-mmm, I'm hungry," I said to Christine. "And Mama is cooking her yummy fried chicken and spaghetti!"

"Yeah, we better hurry before the others get here," Christine said as I parked my car next to the porch and ran inside, slamming the screen door behind us.

Looking back on that rare afternoon playtime reminds me of another memory. When my sisters began school, I'd sit by the front door, eagerly awaiting their return each afternoon. As soon as Mommy's car drove up, I'd jump up and down a few times, crying, "They're home, they're home!" I'd then run up to my sisters as they entered the house, hugging them and pressing my face against their torsos. I remember the look and feel of their pink-and-white gingham school uniforms as I closed my eyes and deeply inhaled, then proclaimed, "You smell like school!" The exchange ended with another deep whiff. I was fascinated by this unfamiliar odor, which I later discovered was from being outdoors in the sun.

If you came home smelling like freshly washed clothes that had been left outdoors to dry, this place called "school" couldn't be so bad, I wagered. In fact, the notion of school was my first real taste of the world I was missing from within the Pagoda's protective walls.

Once I actually began school, my experience, however, was dramatically different than I'd imagined it would be. Looking back on it today, the one memory that arises is palpable since it is a body memory; my stomach feels as though it is in knots at the very thought of my school years. I dreaded the time I would be away from my mother or siblings. During my elementary years, for example, Sundays were the toughest for me since the next day was a school day. When I heard the opening sequence of the television program *60 Minutes* on Sunday evenings, featuring the ticking sound of a stopwatch, I could feel the beginnings of the knot in my stomach.

Since we children were rarely allowed to venture outdoors until we began attending school, we mainly played indoors in the different sections of the house. Often creative and intense, our games would last for several hours as we entered a world of make-believe. The older children commonly made up the story as the game progressed, and each participant stayed in character. We often played Cowboys and Indians, at which time the older kids assigned each child a role and distributed the appropriate gear, either a gun or a bow and arrow. Our games were so engrossing that it's hard to imagine them from an adult perspective, even for me. I can best sum it up in my memory of a particular time when our day-long game ended because it became too real. One of the younger children began to cry because she believed that the enemy camp had really captured some of us.

All under one roof, we were more than just siblings or cousins. We were best friends. We played together, ate together, slept together, and understood life in a unique way that no one, on Guam or anywhere else, could truly relate to. Also, because there were so many of us in the group, we learned to manage our actions, moods, and relationships in a special way. For example, we found that we would only be heard if we spoke quickly and concisely. Failing to do so meant that someone else would seize the group's attention and we would lose our chance of being heard, thus silencing a thought before it even had a chance to catch air.

Life at the Pagoda wasn't all fun and games, however. Like most families during that time, our mothers stayed home while our fathers were away at work. As a result, their control over us and our activities was unrelenting. Silence and discipline were highly prized in the family. The phrase "Children are to be seen, not to be heard" best describes their view of a child's role. Even during family dinners, we understood that we were never to interrupt their conversation. In short, we spoke only when spoken to, no matter the situation. One look from our mothers, with narrowed eyes and pursed lips, was all it would take to put an end to our antics.

More telling, perhaps, was a disciplinary tactic they used. They were diligent about instilling fear, applying this tactic to make sure we would avoid situations or things considered dangerous (as in the case of keeping us away from the tower). This was a method, no doubt, of guaranteeing that we would maintain our good behavior even when left unsupervised—a method that, in many ways, haunted us as we grew.

A great representation of this attitude surrounded the existence of "boonie dogs," or stray dogs, which were rampant on Guam at the time and often traveled in packs. The packs, which typically consisted of three or more dogs, would temporarily settle near people's homes. Perhaps because of the compound's size, this happened often at the Pagoda, and we would periodically come across a new pack. Our mothers deterred us from approaching or playing with the dogs by telling us we'd be bitten. This deterrent proved to be problematic, especially since many of us had no other experience with animals. Whenever we saw a boonie dog

headed our way (or any dog, for that matter), our first reaction
was to run for fear of being attacked. Interpreting this as play,
the dog(s) would naturally follow in pursuit. I remember crying
and screaming for Mommy as we'd run into the house,
slamming the screen door behind us. We would stand by the
door once we were inside, curiously observing the confused,
panting dog on the other side, who seemed to be thinking, *I
don't get this game.*

Our main form of discipline was far less elaborate, however.
Our mothers instituted a careful balance of spankings and
silence. Through these tactics, we quickly learned the difference
between right and wrong. Silence was the most powerful way
of communicating in our family, and it extended far beyond
teaching children right from wrong. Whenever the adults had a
misunderstanding, they would simply not speak with each other
for however long it took for things to cool down, sometimes
several days—or even years, as was the case in the time that
followed our life at the Pagoda.

Silence as a punishment meant that Mommy would completely ignore the culprit. One night as we sat down for dinner,
she turned the Lazy Susan that was attached to our circular
wooden dining table and intermittently stopped when the main
dish—a platter of rib-eye steaks—was in front of my other
siblings at the table. "Go on, get that piece right there in front,"
she'd say to them. "It's a good one!" When my turn came,
Mommy didn't say a word but just stopped it in front of me.
So, I reached out for mine.

"V-very good steak, honey. I feel like I'm eating at the
Hilton!" Daddy said to my mother as he gestured an "OK"
hand signal before taking another hearty bite.

Mommy would continue to ignore the child in question
throughout the meal. As she talked and laughed with everyone

else at the table, I often felt invisible and found myself wondering if maybe this particular transgression was different from all the others. Could it be that Mommy, who loved me more than anyone else did, had experienced a change of heart? The invisibility ended only when we apologized. The banishment was so unbearable that many times, I would have rather endured a spanking than the penetrating isolation of her silence.

CHAPTER FOUR

Breaking Away

Like all childhood bliss, our time as a large multi-generational family all under one roof was fleeting. Once it ended, an equally significant phase of my life began, marked by a stark change in family dynamic. As the new decade approached, the extended family began to slowly disperse, beginning with Auntie's return to the Philippines and Uncle's move to another village on Guam. Shortly thereafter, my parents took five of their children and moved to their first home, which was only a few minutes' drive from the Pagoda, where Jasmine and Glenn remained. It was at this point that my brother Eugene formally resumed living with the immediate family. Though I never learned what transpired to allow this, I did know that Eugene's relationship with Genny had become very close over the years; as a result, he had begun spending a great deal of time with our nuclear family unit rather than with Mama and Papa. I guess since Mommy's other son, Glenn, was to stay on with him, Papa relented and allowed Eugene to return to our family. The move to our new home seemed like the logical time to do this.

My mother underwent a transformation in our new home. Always an unassuming and hardworking homemaker, my mother was a no-nonsense woman who barely wore make-up and dressed in practical cotton shift dresses. Her entrance into our household leadership was not typical for a woman of her standing. Firmly believing it was best to do things herself in order to get them done, her Chinese roots stood firm and she headed into home ownership the only way she knew how: choosing not to have help. She ran our household single-handedly.

Her keen practical sense was further reflected in the design of our new home, which she had planned for years. From the start, she decided on a one-story structure, which, in her opinion, was invaluable in terms of housekeeping. The idea was that it would take less time to maintain if there weren't any stairs to climb. Except for the trim of the roof, which was royal blue, our three-bedroom home was painted white and stood on a one-acre plot with a front yard that took up most of the land. A semi-rectangular row of small pine shrubs separated the premises from the quiet street in front of it. Our home certainly had a more modest exterior than the Pagoda, but it was just as comfortable—perhaps even more so since every room had an air conditioner that ran twenty-four hours a day.

Like many other homes built during that time, ours was made of cement while older homes, such as the Pagoda, were mainly constructed from wood. So, whenever a typhoon swept through the island we rarely suffered damages. And oddly enough, some of my fondest childhood memories were made during such times. In May 1976, for example, "Pamela," one of Guam's most powerful typhoons, slammed the island with winds exceeding one hundred miles per hour. As the rain and gale pummeled the house, we kids sat comfortably in the dining room listening to the sounds of various objects, like garbage cans or heavy tree branches, hurling from time to time onto the sides of our boarded windows. Despite the catastrophe taking place outside and the major damage it was causing to others in our village, we focused on listening to one of our Elton John records playing on the battery-operated phonograph or sketching by candlelight. In every way, my parents had designed our home to protect us, even from the things we could not control, such as the forces of nature.

The one thing about my mother that remained consistent throughout our lives was her storytelling. As we grew older, she spoke more and more about her own childhood during the Japanese occupation of the Philippines. Typically, she began a story during the course of a meal and continued on for hours after we were done eating. Each time, we would remain in our seats with our empty plates in front of us, utterly captivated by her tales of the atrocities of war. Beyond the fact that her stories were delivered with superb timing, intrigue, and her own particular brand of humor, I was especially fascinated to hear her speak from the unique perspective of the ten-year-old child she was at the time.

Thus, aerial combat between fighter planes—or dogfighting, as she called it—was deemed as exciting as if it were done in play. The image of two cartoon-like puppies frolicking against a sky-blue backdrop often came to mind.

"I remember the day Auntie, Uncle and I stood behind this big tree watching the Japanese soldiers firing their machine gun up at the sky, at an American plane flying overhead. Rat-atatat! Rat-atatat!" Mommy exclaimed as she held her hands in front of her as though she were actually maneuvering the gun. "Rat-atatat! Rat-atatat!" she cried again. "We did our best to hide behind a big tree because we knew we'd be in trouble if the Japanese saw us. Then, we saw smoke coming out of the tail of the plane. The next thing we knew, the pilot parachuted out of the plane and landed not too far from the soldiers. We were all saying under our breath, 'Run! Hurry! Run!' But the pilot had landed flat on his back, unconscious. He was a six-footer, I'm sure—so tall and so handsome. He looked like the actor Tyrone Power. So handsome! Later, it took several of the Japanese soldiers to lift the pilot onto their truck. I don't know whatever happened to that pilot. *Ang guwapo!*" She ended in Tagalog, emphasizing how handsome the pilot was.

She was such a gifted storyteller that even though she told them over and over, each tale seemed fresh whenever she told it, as though I were hearing it for the first time. She had a sparkle in her eyes and she seemed to come alive, especially when she spoke of Papa. Mommy always ended her stories by shaking her head and lamenting, "Oh, it seems just like yesterday. The years go by so quickly..." After hearing this, I'd often wonder, *Well, how can it be just like yesterday when it was a long, long time ago?*

Now that we lived apart from Papa, Daddy's time with us became more defined as well. He relished engaging us in actual play and established a role of comrade, a huge departure from Papa's role, or even our mother's. As young children, our favorite game with Daddy was when he'd swing us back and forth between his legs. After each having our turn, it always seemed so easy to convince him that we should have another round. "Just one more time," we'd beg. We knew our turn was over whenever he would bring us up to his face for a quick kiss on the cheek. He was a heavy smoker for most of his life, and my earliest memories of my father always include the smell of tobacco and the image of the ever-present green-and-white pack of Salem cigarettes visible through his shirt pocket.

Indeed, Daddy's personality had always been a great contrast to his wife's, as evidenced by the manner in which their marriage came to pass.

My parents' lengthy courtship began when she was just eighteen. Besides his gentle demeanor, Daddy was strikingly handsome. He stood 5'8" tall with chiseled features, distinctive eyebrows, black hair, and dark eyes that contrasted sharply with his pale skin. One particular photograph of him stands out in my memory. It's a family portrait taken during his bachelor days. In the studio shot, Daddy is seated on a bench along with his brother and his brother's wife. His thick black hair is slicked back and parted on one side. He wears a crisp white shirt with the sleeves folded to his forearms and beige trousers with a clean crease down the center of each leg. A pair of brown-and-white spectator shoes finishes off his sharp, put-together look. When I first came across the photo as an adult, I blurted, "Wow, Daddy, you were gorgeous—you must have broken some hearts!"

Mommy was in the next room, so Daddy looked at me and, with a twinkle in his eyes, muttered, "A few."

"Ooh, I'm going to tell Mommy!" We laughed and looked at each other as though it was our little secret.

My mother was not ready for a serious relationship when they first met, so she didn't actually view my father as a potential mate until years later. This was due, in part, to the fact that he was ten years her senior. Daddy was a patient man, though, so he waited. When she was in her late twenties and the time had come for Mommy to marry, he was there. Daddy once described the courtship period in his life as "the time I fell in love," and it was obvious that, throughout his life, he counted those years as being among his very best. One of the first presents Mommy had given him was a sepia photograph of herself taken in a garden, standing between two tall shrubs with white flowers in full bloom. Pleasingly plump as always, she wears a white cotton dress with a matching chiffon scarf tied as a headband, arranged to pull her wavy bobbed hair away from her face. With the ends of the scarf billowing at her side, her

The photograph of my father that took my breath away.
Daddy is on the right and is pictured along with his brother and his brother's wife.

pretty face seemed to glow in the sunlight. Daddy was a sentimental man, and he would keep this gift tucked away in his wallet for the rest of his life.

"Honey, I'm going to set up the new swing set for the kids," Daddy said one Saturday afternoon. Genny, Eugene, and I stood behind him dressed in our T-shirts, shorts, and rubber zoris, eager to finally get our hands on the playset Daddy had picked up for us earlier that week.

"Yeah, I want to try out the slide!" Eugene exclaimed.

"And we want to play with the swings," Genny and I said in unison.

"What? Oh, no, it's too hot outside right now," Mommy declared.

"Oh, okay," Daddy quietly said as he looked at us with a smile. "Maybe we'll play tomorrow morning."

It's not surprising that with her strength of character equaling Papa's, Mommy was the one who made all the decisions at home. This could be especially frustrating because she sometimes based a decision solely on her mood. Yet this aspect of her character complemented Daddy's passive ways and made our home tick reliably, like an old clock. They were like two parts coming together to make a whole and presented us all with a clear image of partnership in the truest sense.

This portrayal of character and family roles continued into the lives of the five children who moved from the Pagoda into our new home. Each of us played a particular role in the family, and that role was dictated by our personalities and relative placement in the hierarchy of Mommy's "favorites." Joyce was the musician who excelled in piano and singing. My younger sister Genny was the genius who effortlessly got straight A's in school. The artist in the family was Eugene, whose creativity only seemed to flourish with each passing year. And for as far

*Che-Che and me with our mother on the airport's tarmac
in the Philippines, en route to board our flight home to Guam.*

back as I can remember, Jocelyn and I had always simply held the role of being our mother's favorites. These roles were further broken down into distinct sub-roles between the two of us.

As the eldest child, Jocelyn's family nickname is Che-Che, which means "older sister" in Chinese. Since Mommy gave her a certain amount of power, Che-Che fittingly assumed the responsibilities of the "dutiful child," which included delegating to her younger siblings such household tasks as folding laundry and putting away the dishes.

Such chores were assigned to everyone except me. My own role was to be Mommy's other favorite, and I was always treated accordingly.

As the fourth child in a family of seven children, I was smack in the middle with three older sisters before me and three younger siblings after. Contrary to the popular stereotype of the neglected middle child, however, Mommy spoiled me, absolving me of chores except for the task of cleaning up after myself.

Up until about the age of four, I was so attached to Mommy that I even slept between my parents in their bed. My older sisters had also done so; however, they made the gradual transition to their own beds as they grew older. My progression did not come as easily. Therefore, I remained in bed with my parents even when my younger sister Genny's turn came to sleep in between them. For a time, it was the four of us in their king size bed with me, of course, next to Mommy. At one point, it became impossible for me to fall asleep without her by my side, so I would follow my mother around the house until she was ready to come to bed, even if it meant not sleeping until midnight.

As the "pampered child," I was encouraged to stay "plump"

(some would call it overweight) and was often showered with toys (more so than the others). Despite my weight, my mother always made me feel that I was pretty, even to the point of venerating traits that would have otherwise made me self-conscious. For example, I have numerous beauty marks aesthetically concentrated around my mouth. Mommy once told me that having so many moles meant I would always have many admirers. She would even thrust her opinion of me onto others—albeit subtly, as is the Asian way. When she met acquaintances by chance, she would gently prod me towards them and say, "This is my daughter Julie." She would then pause, using silence as her segue. On cue, most would reply, "Oh, what a cute daughter you have—she's going to grow up to be a pretty girl." Mommy would then smile and look at me silently, in a practiced response, her face, nevertheless, beaming with pride.

It wasn't long after we left the Pagoda that Papa made his own move. He and Mama settled in San Francisco along with Jasmine and Glenn. There, he purchased three homes in the city's upscale Marina District. Papa and Mama lived in the main house, a six-bedroom home that we aptly referred to as "the Marina" since it was located directly on the renowned Marina Boulevard. On a small street behind the Marina stood the second house, which was specifically purchased for my parents and the five of us children, should we eventually move to the city. Papa also purchased a third home, located only a couple of miles away, for either Auntie or Uncle in case they decided to move abroad as well.

For the next several years, we spent our summers either in Manila to be near Auntie or in San Francisco to be near Papa. Life in these cities was fast-paced and sophisticated, which made my life on Guam pale in comparison. As I grew older, I began to feel isolated from the rest of the world. For instance, it wasn't until the mid-seventies that cable television came to the island, which meant, to our dismay, that we had only the major network channels, about four in total. Additionally, since they were provided via previously recorded tapes from the mainland, all programs—including the news—were a week behind. We thus mainly kept informed by way of the only local newspaper, the only radio station, and the only local television station.

Once I was exposed to city life, San Francisco became my idea of Shangri-La. During our first trip to the city in 1971, my parents took three of us—Genny, Eugene, and me—for one last drive across the Golden Gate Bridge before our trip home the next day. As we made our way through the early evening traffic jam and crossed the fog-covered bridge, my heart sank. I knew how much I would miss Papa, Mama, Jasmine, and Glenn—and, of course, this city. But then a smile came across my face as the three of us in the back seat stuck our hands out the half-opened windows and attempted to grab the cold mist in our hands.

Giggling, I said, "Daddy, Daddy, can we take some home with us in a jar?"

"Oh no, honey bun," Daddy answered jovially. "We can't take it home."

Although we were unable to grab even a handful, San Francisco would nevertheless remain with me.

CHAPTER FIVE

A Family Tragedy: April 17, 1973

The *Pacific Daily News* headline read, "Corn Dies at 75." The article included a recent black-and-white photograph of Papa in which he appeared to be much older than I remembered. Did he really have so many lines on his face? Was he as gaunt as he seemed to be in that photo? I found it strange, even then, how our feelings distort our memories of people and events. As a larger-than-life influence on my world, Papa had seemed invincible despite the mounting evidence to the contrary.

In fact, Papa's health had been on the decline since the late 1960s, starting with a series of strokes. The last stroke had been a massive one that had occurred during a visit to Taipei in the fall of 1971. Papa had invited thirty guests from Guam, including friends, journalists, and government officials, to accompany him and Mama on an all-expenses-paid trip where he was to accept an honorary doctorate from the China Academy for years of his philanthropic work. My father was always in charge of the businesses whenever Papa was away, so my parents and the five of us were able to join the family only after Papa fell ill. For almost a month thereafter, we, along with some of the original guests, stayed at the Grand Hotel in Taipei until Papa regained enough strength to travel back home. Not long after the family arrived on Guam, Mama, Jasmine and Glenn returned to San Francisco in time for the start of the school year.

After Papa's release from Guam's Naval Hospital, he returned home to the Pagoda. From left, Genny, Eugene and I visiting with him and Mama in their bedroom. 1970.

Even though Papa had hired help to care for him, my mother began to arrange her daily activities around Papa's schedule in order to become his full-time caretaker. So, in addition to running her own household, my mother somehow managed to find the time to personally care for him at the Pagoda. But to my mother, this unyielding devotion was only what any dutiful daughter should do for her ailing father.

A typical day for my mother was as follows: she would get the five of us up and ready for the day, drive us to school, and then spend the rest of the morning and early afternoon at the Pagoda cooking, cleaning, doing laundry, and completing other chores. She would then fetch us from school and prepare our meals, returning to the Pagoda in the evening to prepare Papa's dinner. Once he settled each evening, she then returned home to ensure that we were ready for the next school day. She went on like this for a couple years, living in monotony.

At some point, my siblings and I took turns staying overnight at the Pagoda on weekends. On one rare occasion, Papa and I were the only ones at home—his nurse and secretary were out, perhaps running errands. As I did my homework in the bedroom, I realized it had been some time since Papa went to the kitchen for a glass of water so I decided to look for him. But he was nowhere to be found. It was always a strange and surely rare experience to hear complete silence at the Pagoda. Stranger still, that afternoon the silence was so intense that the air seemed stagnant, almost stifling. I began to worry.

During my search, I found that one of the house's side doors had been left open, but the screen door was closed. I remember walking as close to the screen as I could, until my nose pressed against it. There I saw Papa strolling on the concrete walkway that ran alongside the house, heading towards the main entrance. The day was drab, but the blazing sun was slowly breaking through the clouds and haze. He was dressed in his customary white Oxford shirt and gray silk trousers. I was struck by the whiteness of his thick hair, which appeared to have the same intensity as the color of his shirt. He walked with his back turned to me, his arms behind him with one hand lightly clutching the other. Papa's walk was slow and unsteady as he stopped from time to time to look at the house from where he stood. He would tilt his head as far back as possible, then slowly move his gaze down the structure, as if he were soaking in every detail. He walked several yards and continued this curious ritual. As I stood there, a warm breeze filtered through the screen door and I was filled with an emotion I'd never known.

I felt an overwhelming sadness that I, a ten-year-old, couldn't possibly understand. Here was a self-made man who, through hard work and determination, had acquired much more than he probably ever dreamed possible. Still, he had now perhaps come to realize that he ultimately had no control over certain matters, like death, regardless of what he did—including renovating the Pagoda.

Like his life, Papa's death was one of fable and grandeur. While at a party on April 17, 1973, Papa suffered a massive heart attack right at the dinner table. As everyone stood for a toast, Papa fell onto his chair, clutched his chest, then gripped the armrests and lost consciousness. His personal nurse—who sat beside him—quickly administered nitroglycerin under his tongue, but to no avail. Doctors pronounced him dead at 10:30 p.m. at Guam Memorial Hospital, and my life on the island changed forever.

Interestingly, Papa's death didn't have as strong of an impact on me as one would think. His presence in my life had always been tangential, and as one of my mother's children who was *not* chosen to live with him, my presence in his life was likely viewed much in the same way. The sadness I experienced upon his death was for my mother since her role as favorite child mimicked my own role within our nuclear family.

At his request, we buried Papa on a hilltop on a remote 1,200-acre piece of land he had acquired soon after the war. Getting to the site entailed driving through curvy, rocky terrain before reaching the very top, which had a sweeping view of the island. As he'd instructed, his final resting place was a cement tomb six feet under the ground. For the actual burial, we slowly made our way up the treacherous hill, using a makeshift tin roof to shield the site itself. However, like all things that stood for my grandfather, his burial plot would have a grand makeover in the ensuing months. Early on, plans were in place to pave the rocky road leading to the site and, to ease our traveling burden, a small house would be constructed for our stays there. Finally, a cement roof would be constructed over the tomb, designed to look like a small-scale replica of the Pagoda. It was a last and fitting homage to my grandfather that, even in death, we made sure to surround him with comfort and family.

As we children stood underneath the tin roof at the graveside, we quietly cried while listening to the women wailing, in both Tagalog and Chinese, "Papa...Pa....why?" Mommy was on the other side of the casket. She wore a black short-sleeved shift dress and knelt on the concrete surface by the closed casket, her face covered by the black chiffon scarf she wore over her head. As the casket was closed and slowly lowered into the tomb, she pulled the scarf from her head and held it in her hands, sobbing even harder. Her tortured cries seemed to come from the very depths of her soul. It was agony in its rawest form. Her wails of anguish and despair at the burial haunted my eleven-year-old mind to such an extent that, despite everything I have been through in my life since, her cries of pain and suffering are still with me today. I was so shocked to see my mother in such a helpless state that I found myself focusing on her bare legs, wondering if kneeling on the hard surface was painful.

In retrospect, Papa's funeral was when I first noticed the place in each one of us that holds our sorrows, a place that is only accessible during times of great loss. In my family, which prided itself on decorum and the art of knowing when to say nothing, this display of emotion seemed especially significant. The realities of my surroundings drowned this epiphany, but the lesson was not only learned but imprinted upon me as I saw the depth of feelings surrounding me that hot afternoon.

Once the casket reached the bottom of the tomb, one of my uncles yelled, "Here, throw a flower in and say your last goodbyes!" He thrust in front of us a bucket filled with long-stemmed pink carnations.

"Hurry, before they close it. Hurry, get one!" His sense of urgency only escalated the pandemonium, and the screaming and cries intensified as everyone began their final farewells. I was so frightened by the chaos that I feared falling into the grave myself, which would have been easy since the younger grandchildren stood at the very edge. More frightening still was the notion that, wrapped in grief, perhaps no one would notice. Throughout the service, I stood as still as I could, focused more on the weight of my feet than on what people were saying, hoping desperately that doing so would plant me firmly to my spot. I came to my senses at the last possible moment, however. I clutched my carnation to my chest and whispered, "Goodbye, Papa," hoping he would hear. Finally, with my arm extended over the grave, I unclasped my hand and watched my carnation fall on top of what was now a mound of flowers.

In the weeks and months following his death, the hole left by my grandfather's passing was gaping and obvious. Perhaps no one grieved over him more than my own mother. It was the first time I had ever seen Mommy in such a vulnerable and helpless state. Over the next year, she frequently broke down crying. "I miss my father," she'd say. Yet she wanted no reminders of him; they were simply too painful to bear. Because she wanted none of his treasured mementos from the Pagoda, everything my grandfather owned and loved was divided among other relatives. My mother wore black for two years after his death, and from then on stopped attending mass on a regular basis. In her grief, she seemed to have lost faith in a God that had taken someone whom she had loved so dearly.

Without Papa, the family would never be the same. Soon after his passing, we learned that he had left two last wills and testaments, one in Guam and another in Hong Kong. This period finally brought the concept of his "second family," his wife and another son, to the forefront of all of our lives for the first time. Despite his impression of a larger-than-life influence, like us all, Papa's choices came to call once he met his end. The situation forced our family to deal with what they had, in many ways, chosen to silence for decades—and without him there to act as support.

As the appointed executors of the Guam estate, my parents became embroiled in a legal battle with the Hong Kong family. Differences as to how the situation should be handled then arose between my parents and both Uncle and Auntie, and the internal dispute got out of control. This resulted in a silence between family members that lasted several years. The worst part about this time was that, just as we needed them most, my siblings and I lost all contact with our childhood friends and the only other people who understood just how profoundly the actions of the adults around us, including Papa, impacted us as young children: our cousins.

One afternoon, my mother picked the five of us up from school and took us to McDonald's for a quick bite to eat before shopping at Town House just across the street. Suddenly, Mommy said, "Uncle and Freddie just walked in. Don't look at them." I was sitting beside my mother and was facing the front door, so I had also seen them as they walked in. Following my mother's instructions to not look, I sat motionless and forced myself to stare straight ahead towards the windows. I focused on the packed parking lot outside, but I could still see them from the corner of my eye. Uncle walked past, looking straight ahead at the order counter, as our younger cousin Freddie—who must have been about six years old at the time—walked closely behind him. I imagined that Freddie wore his favorite wristwatch, the one that was almost identical to his father's. He had both his hands in his pant pockets, just as his dad always did.

"Hurry up and finish eating. We'll be leaving soon," Mommy said minutes later, looking specifically at me. It was then that I saw, to my surprise, the half-eaten sandwich that lay before me.

We were simply told by our parents never to speak with our cousins again, even if we were to encounter each other on the street. By then, the adults' way of resolving things through silence had become an accepted and ordinary part of our lives. We followed their instructions without question, and without recognizing the profound impact it had on us.

To make matters even more terrible for me, it was shortly thereafter that Che-Che and I stopped speaking with one another. From the very start, our situation distressed Mommy, who could not comprehend how her Favorites could dislike each other. Indeed, she was not one to allow such dramatics to continue and made some futile attempts to intervene. She once forced us to sit together in an armchair, yelling, "I've had enough of this! I want the two of you to talk to each other, NOW!" Despite the seriousness of her words, neither of us complied. I remember quickly pulling myself away from Che-Che and felt her doing the same, so that we had as little body contact as possible. As we sat there with our noses defiantly pointed in the air, we refused to look at one another.

Perhaps our mother was never able to resolve our differences because lecturing us on how sisters should love one another might have brought up her own troubled relationship with Auntie—her only sister. She didn't lecture us at all because it was too painful for her. At the time, my mother seemed unfazed by her estrangement with Auntie, and like her, I may have appeared to be unaffected by the way things had turned out between Che-Che and me. But, in truth, there were many times when I was overwhelmed by a strange and uncomfortable feeling. I experienced intense moments of sadness over the matter, and it took great effort at times for me to maintain our detachment. I would have to remind myself that we were not like ordinary sisters, who acknowledged one another. A part of me deep within sensed this type of relationship was unnatural—a fact that was confirmed years later, after my mother and Auntie reconciled. My mother later spoke of a similar anguish. The pervasive silence may have only compounded her grief over losing Papa.

CHAPTER SIX

A Beautiful Mask

"Please, Mommy, please let Julie come with me," Jasmine cried.

Shortly after Papa's funeral, I accompanied my parents to the airport for Mama, Jasmine, and Glenn's journey back home to San Francisco. My sister and I had grown much closer that summer and the idea came to us as we began our goodbyes at the airport's coffee shop. It started off with "I'm going to miss you" and "I wish I could go with you." Then Jasmine concluded, "You should come with us!" Later, when we summoned the courage to broach the matter with our mother, we approached her by the ticket counter. Jasmine stood at one side, pleading as best she could: "Please, Mommy, please let Julie come with us, please." I stood on the other side, holding my mother's arm, and sobbed. "Please, Mommy, please let me go with Jasmine!"

"Are you crazy?" Our mother at first dismissed us. "You are not going anywhere!"

The airport's intermittent PA announcements shrieked in the background, which only increased my sense of urgency. We had to convince our mother before it was time for Jasmine to board, or worse still, before our mother became so annoyed that she'd reject the matter altogether.

"Please, Mommy," Jasmine finally cried. "Please let Julie come with me so I won't be so lonely." My mother subtly tilted her head and her eyes shifted, as though Jasmine's words—"so I won't be so lonely"—had made all the difference.

"Okay," our mother eventually relented. "You can go, but you have *one year only*." She leaned down and looked me squarely in the eye. "Do you understand me?" my mother asked, holding her index finger to my face. "One year!"

"Yes, Mommy, yes—one year!" I felt as though a weight had been lifted off me; my head and chest suddenly felt lighter. One whole year in San Francisco with my sister was like a dream come true. *We did it,* I thought. *We really did it.*

My mother then turned to my father. "Lee, go home and get her passport and a jacket! I'll buy her ticket."

And so it was that at age eleven, I moved to San Francisco for "one year only," as dictated by my mother. Looking back, I'm certain her decision stemmed from her concern for Jasmine more than from my own protestations. For Jasmine, Papa's loss was much more like my mother's since he had stood in as her father figure. My mother's logic, I assume, was that it was not a good idea to keep Jasmine so isolated from the rest of the family, and especially her sisters, so soon after losing Papa.

Whatever the intention, this choice was truly my gain since my bond with Jasmine had always been strong. Indeed, Jasmine and I shared a special connection from the very start. Although I am three years her junior, there is only one day between our birthdays—Jasmine's is on March 10th and mine is on the 12th. We are both Pisces and share the common characteristics of that astrological sign. In fact, our family has always attributed our common love for things that are pretty and feminine— dresses, jewelry, and anything else that defines the perennial female—to our shared Piscean nature. Throughout that year in San Francisco, our bond deepened during such a turbulent time in both our lives.

Although my parents had sheltered me on Guam, while abroad, my relationship with my "parent," Mama, was indifferent. It had always been that way between us and was a welcome departure from the burden of my role on Guam. Just as my mother had always favored Che-Che and me, it was clear that Jasmine and Glenn came first to my grandmother. Because it had always been this way, it never bothered me. Besides, there were other women living with us at the time who, in combination, might have represented mother figures to me. There was Tia Nitz, a distant aunt who served as Mama's secretary and confidante; she was also adept at addressing the practical matters in my life such as ensuring that my homework was done at the end of the day. Then there was Coring, our cook, who mainly kept to herself but nurtured me with her succulent delicacies. And finally, there was Lita, who was, in retrospect, the main reason for my successful adjustment to life without my mother. Lita had been our nanny during the early years at the Pagoda, but we children viewed her more as a beloved family member. Because of my intense attachment to my mother in my early years, it wasn't until my move to San Francisco that I came to know and love Lita like the others did.

Although Lita would eventually leave our family to return home to the Philippines, she has always remained with us by instilling the true nature of unconditional love. She showered us with hugs and kisses, and it is Lita's deep affection for us that stands out most in my memories of her. Hers was indeed a kind of love unlike any other. She appeared to love each one of us equally, a quality that the other women in my family seriously lacked. This unconditional love affected me more than I knew at the time. Although she primarily cared for Glenn by the time I arrived in San Francisco, I never felt Lita favored him in any way. I was always calm with Lita. She offered an understanding presence that no one else has ever supplied for me in quite the same way.

One Saturday afternoon, Jasmine arrived home from a shopping expedition with Tia Nitz. "Look, Julie, I got us the purses we wanted!" Jasmine said. She removed two handbags from a large shopping bag. She positioned them side by side on the dining table. "I know you wanted the smaller purse," she said, "but when I opened it, it was really too small to fit anything, so I got you the same size as the one I got. I sure hope you like it! It doesn't have leather stitching on the edges like mine does, so it doesn't look as big as the one I got, and it's roomy enough but not too big for you." Jasmine held the purse between us.

I hung the long leather strap over my shoulder and declared, "Wow, I love it! It's exactly like the ones your friends at school have."

Besides the idea that the purse was popular among the older girls at Jasmine's high school, it was almost identical to the one our idol at the time, Cher, carried in a picture we'd come across in a *Photoplay* magazine.

"It looks very nice on you. It's the perfect size," Tia Nitz concurred.

"Now, remember, Mama wants to go out for Japanese food tonight, and our reservation is at six." Tia Nitz quickly added, "We have about an hour, so the two of you better shower now and get ready." Tia Nitz always ensured we were on schedule for our day.

Coring—our cook—stepped into the dining room and interjected. "Jasmine and Julie, you didn't have any of the *pan de sal* I baked this morning," she said. "Would you like to have some before you get ready?"

"No," Jasmine responded, casting a glance my way. "Maybe later."

Although Coring's freshly baked bread rolls were usually the best part of our Saturdays, neither my sister nor I were interested because we were simply too excited about our new handbags.

"Come on, Jas," I said as we ran out of the dining room and headed up the stairs to our bedroom, new shoulder bags in tow. "Let's see if we can find something to wear with our purses!"

"Shh!" Lita hushed us when we reached the top of the stairs. She was heading towards the bedroom with four-year-old Glenn cradled in her arms. He was sound asleep, and I was surprised at how big my brother appeared to be in her arms. It seemed as if he was half of Lita's diminutive size. As we followed her into the bedroom, Lita murmured, "I've put out towels for your shower. I'm going to get him to bed for his nap, so don't make too much noise." She gently placed Glenn into bed.

Scenes like this make my time in San Francisco seem mundane, and it was—but I appreciated every moment of it. As much as my love for my sister and her need for companionship brought me to the city, it was San Francisco herself, in all of her sensory glory, that gave me the sustenance I needed to thrive during that year. The cold climate, especially the fog, was a constant reminder that I was far from home, in a new life—a world without my mother's dominating presence. More than anything, however, it is the sounds of San Francisco which most accurately capture my time spent there in the 1970s and illustrate the rapid physical and emotional transformation that took place throughout that time. The cable car bells, for instance, reflected the pulse of the city, which excited my own. It was riveting and full of life. In striking contrast were the foghorns, which touched a deeper, more spiritual part of me. I left my window halfway open each night at bedtime so that I was lulled to sleep by the sounds of that deeply soothing, hypnotic cry of the foghorn, which gave the same comfort I'd felt as a small child when my mother would softly hum as I fell asleep in her arms.

It wasn't just the city herself that called to me, however, but my place within it. Mundane sounds such as the hardwood floors creaking underneath me as I made my way around the 1920s structure I now called home reminded me each day that, on some level, I was surely a part of this world. I had a view of San Francisco Bay, Alcatraz, Angel Island, and the Golden Gate Bridge from its various windows. Our house was located on Marina Boulevard in the heart of that bustling city, and one of its largest appeals was its location. Right in the middle of San Francisco, we existed in a place and time where much was starting to happen.

Living at the Marina was such a dramatic departure from my relatively quiet existence on Guam, whereby our concrete home and the ever-present hum of air conditioners had, for years, kept us well insulated. In fact, the whole of my life in San Francisco was undoubtedly different than the one I'd left behind. It was here, in San Francisco, that I began to relate to the world outside of my family. No longer the shy and chubby kid in class, I made fast friends with my new classmates—both girls and boys—and was even selected by my peers to play the lead part in a class production of *Cinderella*.

My best friends, Heather and Bettina, came to the Marina with me after school one day. We were thrilled to have completed our homework with enough time to play outside before their return home. "Don't go off too far," Tia Nitz told us as we ran out the front door. We ran through the crosswalk to the Marina Green, the large expanse of grass across the street from the homes on Marina Boulevard. "Let's go over there by the boats," Heather said.

We raced across the Green and headed straight to the yacht club walkway, which was lined by rows of boats moored to floating walkways that branched off from the main walkway. When we took a seat, I felt the sting of the cold surface through my denim jeans. I was glad that Tia Nitz had convinced me to wear my heavy jacket. The seagulls' distant cries were punctuated by the curious sounds of boats bobbing in the water, like chimes blowing in the wind. I dangled my feet over the water and rested my chin on the rail in front of me, holding it tightly with both hands, but then saw that my friends held their arms outstretched in front of them.

"Look, it's like we're flying," Bettina said. "Come on, Julie. Put your hands out in front of you like this and look down."

"No, I'm afraid to let go," I said. "What if I fall in the water?" I looked below me at the lapping water of the Bay.

"You won't fall because you'll be leaning against the bar," Bettina reassured me. "You see?" She leaned in even farther and brought her head over the railing so that she was face down.

"Come on, Julie, you can do it," Heather yelled, "Just let go!"

I pressed my chest against the bar. Once I felt its secure hold, I released my tight grip and joined them as we held our arms and legs out in front of us.

"Whee, we're flying!" I exclaimed, laughing.

We remained seated on the walkway, chatting while dangling and kicking our legs over the water.

"Miss Matsumoto was upset by the way Joe and Danny behaved today, talking in class and all," Heather shared. "She said she's never had such disobedient students before."

Glenn and me at the Marina. 1974.

"Really?" Bettina asked, "Is that true, Julie? How were the kids at your old school? Did they misbehave?"

"The kids were the same as the ones in our class," I responded. "Some misbehaved more than others."

"Oh good, so it's just not our class," Bettina said in relief.

I enjoyed my newfound independence and relished the novel idea of having friends outside the family. My friendships were, of course, complemented by my close relationship with Jasmine. She frequently invited me to join her and her high school friends, never seeing her younger sister as a burden. I was still young, though, and there were also plenty of times when I was perfectly content staying at home and playing with Glenn.

My time in San Francisco was my introduction to the world outside my family, but it was also the period when I began to take note of what was going on in the world at large—from the vantage point of San Francisco in the 1970s, no less. It was as if my eyes and ears were opening for the very first time. Patty Hearst became a household name during that year. I also noticed how many young adults in the city's streets looked like characters straight out of my favorite movie, *Jesus Christ Superstar*. Jasmine and I bought the film's soundtrack and played it incessantly on the 8-track in the family's Cadillac, much to our driver's dismay.

Richard Nixon's involvement in the Watergate scandal was also at its height during my time on the mainland, and the incident became embedded in my memory as a turning point which, I later found, defined not only my own understanding of the world but also much of my generation's.

The most significant effect that stemmed from my time in San Francisco was more far-reaching than enhanced personal relationships, though. The mask I had worn as an awkward young girl who was her mother's favorite back on Guam began to slowly peel away and the strong woman I would one day become started to appear in bursts that I didn't quite understand.

For starters, my year abroad marked the end of the period that I like to describe as my Awkward Years. A childhood experience that is common to us all, these years were significant to me because my physical development went a bit awry as my body considered how it would alter itself from girl to woman. I continued to be plump, and my weight had a detrimental effect on my face. My chubby cheeks made my eyes appear scrunched—Awkward Years, indeed! However, all of this changed once I moved abroad. Fortunately, my development took a different course, and within the short span of a year, I blossomed into a tall and slim adolescent, reaching my adult height of 5'6".

Not surprisingly, I took great pride in my body image from this point on. It wasn't long before I began shopping for a new wardrobe that was more grown-up in style since I could now wear the junior line, or even the women's petite collection. I would wear jeans, a sweater, and hiking boots during the day. For more formal occasions, I preferred basic pants and tops with low-heeled shoes. During my year in San Francisco, I bought my very first pair of designer shoes, a wedge pump by Charles Jourdan. At some point, Tia Nitz also accompanied me to Vidal Sassoon, where I agreed to have my overgrown shag cut into a chin-length bob. My new hairdo had much cleaner lines. Rather than silently fading into the background, my new look cemented my metamorphosis into the pretty adolescent San Francisco had helped me become.

CHAPTER SEVEN

Returning Home

My remarkable physical transformation continued when I returned to Guam from San Francisco—accelerated, even.

When I was in my twenties, I reunited with Alan, a once-aspiring fashion designer who had been a good friend during my teenage years in Guam.

"When I saw you, your sisters, and your cousins walk into Juliana's, you all stood out from the rest of the crowd. But when I saw *you*, my mouth dropped open. Oh, Julie," Alan said, shaking his head and remembering that night at the local discotheque, which was part of a London-based chain. "You'll never know what an impact you made on me."

Pausing briefly, Alan leaned back in his chair and sighed, as if he were back in that moment all those years ago. Then he excitedly moved on.

"You were wearing this black tunic with thin gold piping that ran through the top edge and tied as a bow over one shoulder." From time to time, Alan would use his hands to describe his recollection of my outfit. "The tunic gathered at the waist," he said, placing both of his hands on his waistline. "The tunic fell right above the knee, and underneath it, you had on black, slim, pegged pants. You were carrying a gold metal evening clutch bag embossed with small leaves, and of course your shoes, by Charles Jourdan—gold, stiletto-heeled sandals with leather straps over the toes and straps that tied around the ankles." This time Alan used his index finger to draw in the air the crisscross design of the straps that had been wrapped around my ankles. He didn't seem to take a breath as he moved on. "Your hair was pulled back in a chignon and your make-up was dark and smoky around the eyes."

Alan summed up his recollection by saying, "And I thought to myself, 'Where did these people come from? They can't be from around here.' I later learned you were only fifteen—an Academy girl—and you were all the late Charlie Corn's grandchildren. I then remember thinking to myself, 'Well, I guess there's no chance of my ever getting to know them.'" Shaking his head, as if in disbelief that so much time had lapsed, Alan stared into the distance as though he had been transported back in time. He ended with, "Oh, Julie, you'll *never* know what an impact you made on me!"

Besides possessing a keen interest in fashion, our attention to detail was another thing that drew us together. Alan quickly became my best friend and would even accompany me to handpick my outfits during my shopping sprees. I could clearly recall the occasion he referred to, for it exemplified our evenings out. As we walked into the disco that night, it had felt as though the crowd cleared a path for my cousins and me. We always seemed to breeze through a crowded room.

By the time I met Alan, my older sisters and I had become young women who looked much older and sophisticated than our years; some even referred to us as the "pretty Lee girls."

We remained very much a unit as well. For someone outside the family to befriend one of us, the others would have to accept that person as well. People marveled at the close resemblance among us girls, which was further emphasized by the way we dressed and fixed ourselves. At a quick glance, many people found it difficult to differentiate between sister and sister—or even cousin and cousin, for that matter. We had diligently learned the art of makeup; our style was influenced by the Saint Laurent models of the late 1970s. Their signature look included eyes lined with kohl pencil and dark shadow brushed slightly upwards at the outer corners.

Makeup was, in fact, something I had been fascinated with for some time. My older cousin, Rebecca—also a Piscean—was adept at applying makeup and had begun coaching me during my first year back on Guam. However, I was just twelve at the time, so I could only listen to my twenty-year-old cousin's expert advice on the matter rather than applying it.

"Hey guys, come over here and sit with me while I get ready," Rebecca called to us from her bedroom. While Joyce remained in the living room with our mother and younger siblings, Che-Che and I came into the room (albeit separately since we were not on speaking terms). We were at Rebecca's house to pick her up on our way to lunch. Rebecca sat at her brightly lit vanity table as she dressed. She wore a red silk Chinese embroidered robe that was tightly tied at the waist, and a towel was wrapped around her wet hair. I took my seat at one of the chairs positioned on each side of the table.

"So, what did I tell you guys this was, again?" Rebecca asked as she held up a small glass bottle filled with beige liquid.

"Foundation!" I quickly proclaimed.

I glanced at Che-Che, who looked at Rebecca through the aviator eyeglasses that hung low on her nose. Her head was tilted back and the rim of her braces was slightly visible. My sister looked bored and not at all bothered that she wasn't the first to answer.

"Good, Julie! That's right," Rebecca replied. "And remember, foundation is the base for the rest of your makeup—with it, the face becomes like an artist's canvas." I sat up and smiled broadly, proud that the subject matter came easily to me.

By the time I was fifteen, my skills in applying make-up were still in their infancy. Thus, there were times when I might have overdone the desired effect. On such occasions, my mother would prohibit me from leaving the house unless I toned it down. Even though I knew she would always have the last word, I'd argue with her anyway. "This is the way it's supposed to look," I'd defiantly reply. After all, what did she know about the Saint Laurent look? There always came a point when dealing with my mother, however, when I knew her mind was made up and nothing I could do or say would alter her decision; my protests would instead only lessen my chances of getting what I wanted. I knew I had reached this point when she commanded, "If you want to go out tonight, you'd better get back in your room *now* and lighten that makeup!" Defeated, I would run into my bedroom, crying, "You never let me do anything!" It typically took several attempts before she approved of the changes.

Since I placed a heavy emphasis on body image, my passion for clothes was at an all-time high. Spending hundreds of dollars each week, I mainly shopped at one of the island's few designer boutiques, Courrèges. It exclusively stocked French designer André Courrèges' stylish resort wear line in colors like fuchsia, pink, and orange in knits and linens. With the limited options available on the island, I was later thrilled to discover a local seamstress who could miraculously recreate pieces from fashion magazines.

During the day, my outfits included a wide-brimmed straw hat with color-coordinated handbag, belt, and shoes. Such extremes were important since a fashion faux pas would be, for example, if my shoes were a different color than my belt.

Dressing became such an intense experience that my mood was often dictated by how satisfied I was with the outcome of my efforts. If my hair did not turn out the way I wanted, I would curse under my breath as I walked out of the house. Many times, I would be in tears while I sat on my closet floor, rejected pieces scattered about me, simply because I was unable to come up with *the* perfect outfit.

Despite my forward-looking wardrobe and desire for the "new," I was still sheltered from life's realities. As my sisters and I grew older, this meant our mother focused specifically on protecting us from boys. The one rule she emphasized above all was that we were not allowed to date until graduating from college (a standard that did not, of course, apply to our brothers). Unbeknownst to our mother, Jasmine, who remained with Mama in San Francisco, had begun dating long before that time. But since hers was a life outside of ours, there was only so much Mommy could do, especially from such a distance. In fact, by the time my mother found out, Jasmine's relationship had bloomed into a serious romance beyond the control of decorum and "rules." Che-Che was the only one among the five girls who diligently complied with this rule, even throughout her college years.

Since my mother was fully aware of my rebellious nature, she was particularly concerned about me. Luckily, it was soon after returning home from my year abroad that we reunited with our cousins, which opened the door for some semblance of freedom without the worry of unwanted male attention. For instance, Mommy allowed me to go out dancing on the weekends when I was escorted by any one of my older male cousins.

My cousins served as confidantes and protectors as well as mentors, and my reunion with them could not have come at a better time. They were in their early twenties, and my mother entrusted them with my care, apparently without consideration. The fact that they, too, were quite young and could therefore readily empathize with an adolescent who was eager to play grown-up was simply my gain.

This was in the late 1970s, the Disco Era, and most of our weekends were spent at Juliana's. Appearing and behaving much older and more sophisticated than I was, the management never questioned me even though the legal drinking age on the island was 18. My cousins frequently allowed me to smoke and drink along with them, and the management blatantly ignored the seemingly minor detail of my age. At my birthday celebrations, they'd casually inquire, "So how old are you now, 16?" I would respond only with a smile.

My cousins set limits for me when necessary, and they were especially overprotective. They firmly told me when I'd had enough to drink, for example, and, out of respect for them, I always obliged when they cut me off. I held a special regard for them. I believed they were at a unique position in their lives; they were young enough to understand the needs and concerns of someone my age, and yet they were also old enough to know the difference between right and wrong. I never perceived their occasional interventions as an attack or as an attempt to dampen my evening. Rather, I saw it as their way of saying that certain behaviors were inappropriate for anyone, regardless of age.

While I enjoyed the benefits of my male cousins' company, my mother's rationale for this arrangement was that, should the need arise, they would be able to protect me physically. More importantly, however, I'm sure she believed their mere presence would deter any potential suitors. And it worked. I was never approached by strangers because I always sat at a

table surrounded by my cousins and their friends. The only
time I was out of their sight was when I would go to the ladies'
room, and even then, my escort for the evening would
accompany me to the door, wait for me outside, and insist that
I hold onto his arm as he walked me back to our table.

Perhaps because of this strict arrangement, I was a late
bloomer regarding my sexuality. My mother's concerns were
unwarranted because I wasn't the least bit interested in boys. In
my view, dating was something for the future. Besides, I was
perfectly content just being introduced to the social scene and
the world of the twenty-something set. And what better time in
history was there to encounter such an interesting and diverse
group of people than the 1970s? Some were into drugs or
heavy drinking, while others were either "fashion plates" or
"fashion victims." There were also many gay men within our
circle of friends.

Homosexuality had always been an issue that was openly
discussed in the family, and by our mothers in particular. It was
never viewed from a moral or social stance. The topic would
come up rather matter-of-factly over the normal course of
conversation: "Oh, so-and-so is gay." Also, for as far back as I
can remember, my mother and Auntie had their hair done by a
young man who was not only openly gay but also possessed a
flamboyant personality. "Boots" confused me at first because,
although I knew he was a man, he acted like a woman in many
ways. Besides having eyebrows that were shaped in a
dramatically high arch, he always wore shoes similar to the
women's go-go boots that were the rage of the day—thus his
nickname, I assumed. Moreover, his steps were small and
delicate when he walked across the beauty shop, as though he
were walking a tightrope. What struck me the most about him,
however, was the manner in which he spoke. In the course of

conversation, his responses were overemphasized: "R-R-R-Really...O-O-H, I know what you MEAN!" What's more, the intonation of his words operated in unison with the expression on his face, such as the widening of his eyes, which left Mommy, Auntie, and Boots in hysterics. Observing him helped me to realize that although he looked different, Boots was just like everyone else. He was a friend to my mother and aunt, and I sought the same sort of friendships for myself.

During my provocative teens, gay men were the perfect companions for me. They fulfilled my mother's golden requirements and made my cousins happy, too. Gay men weren't interested in me sexually and, if needed, could protect me physically. At such an impressionable age, these men—such as my good friend Alan—proved to be a major force in my life. Dazzled by my sense of style, they showered me with compliments and made me feel beautiful when I needed it most. I basked in their mere presence.

Ever since the one glorious year I had spent abroad in San Francisco, I wanted nothing more than to return home to the city. But as was the tradition in our family, we received our one-way passage to live with Mama in the States only after completing high school. As part of the graduating class of 1980, I wondered if the year itself would ever arrive. The beginning of the new decade sounded more like something out of science fiction than something that was, in fact, only a couple of years away. I longed for the independence I'd experienced while living apart from my mother. Back home on Guam, I felt stifled.

"Okay, who did you see tonight?" Mommy inquired when I came home one night, as she always did, no matter the hour.

"Alan, Joe, Toni, and Linda were there," I replied. My mother leaned in even closer so that she was only inches away from my face. It was always understood that I'd reek of

The rebellious teen: With one of my twenty-something friends,
Joe, who was screened and approved by my mother. Guam 1978.

cigarettes since, like everyone else during that time, all my cousins were smokers. Instead, she attempted to detect the smell of alcohol on my breath, which I'd already addressed on the car ride home by consuming vast amounts of Tic Tacs.

Upon graduating from high school, both Che-Che and Joyce had automatically—without question—received their independence by moving to San Francisco for college, away from our mother's watchful eye. While Che-Che remained the ever-dutiful daughter, Joyce, much to everyone's complete surprise, decided after only a year to drop out of college and marry. My mother couldn't stop it because she was powerless from a distance, which had been previously proven when she couldn't stop Jasmine from dating as a teenager. Just as in Jasmine's case, my mother acquiesced to Joyce's decision without much of a fight. The actual physical distance might have only reminded my mother that there were indeed things about our lives she simply could not control. To me, this was exactly the freedom I craved, but to my overprotective mother, it was a dangerous warning sign.

Joyce's behavior was grossly out of character. She was a shy and timid girl who, as a teen, barely wore make-up. It wasn't unusual to find my older sister dressed in a bathrobe watching *The Late Show* on TV as I'd be preparing for a night out. If a daughter like her could break the one rule that dominated our lives, my mother assumed the likelihood of me doing the same was almost guaranteed. Joyce's situation reinforced the different ideas my mother and I held about the probable outcome of my own move. Thus, her concerns about me falling astray continued as strong as ever, reaching a peak with my sister's news.

"When it's time for you to go to college, don't ever think that you can have a boyfriend," she'd remark at times, "because

I would never allow it." Although my mother never elaborated on how she intended to carry this out, I was convinced that she'd find a way to ensure it didn't happen. I was, after all, her Favorite.

Despite my attitude towards dating and romantic relationships, my mother's negative emphasis on the subject and my natural rebellious nature caused me to view "dating" as something to be achieved as I grew older. College became a means of attaining that goal—I didn't see it as a way to have a career or to be financially independent since my family would always take care of me. Rather, being in a relationship and ultimately getting married were the only ways I could see to ever be free of my mother's control.

As promised, I was set for my move upon my graduation in 1980. However, there was one major change from the way my older sisters had departed. My mother announced that I'd be receiving proper supervision while in college because my parents and younger siblings would move to San Francisco along with me—to live with Mama, my older sisters, and Glenn at the Marina. Although I was devastated at first, I quickly got over my disappointment since I was thrilled to be returning to my city. How could I stay angry and silent when I was returning to my Shangri-La?

CHAPTER EIGHT
SAN FRANCISCO

Moving to San Francisco "for college" was indeed a pretense because it was never about scholastic achievements for me. On the contrary, the one major change in my life was that while I continued to go out and have fun, I could now do so in what I considered to be the most beautiful city in the world.

"Fag hag" and "fruit fly" were terms commonly used during this time to describe heterosexual women who surrounded themselves with gay men—in short, someone like me. My dislike of straight clubs stemmed from reasons far more complicated than the fact that many of my friends were gay. I didn't care much for the music they played, but, more importantly, I had no interest whatsoever in the kind of men who frequented such places. These were the types who had difficulty accepting a simple "no" for an answer, although turning down some of the more arrogant ones with my indifference and total lack of interest understandably appealed to the rebel in me. Besides, my gay and straight friends also preferred frequenting San Francisco's gay clubs.

One of our favorites was a two-story warehouse, the Trocadero Transfer. It was located in the South of Market neighborhood, which was mainly an industrial area at the time. The dance club opened in 1977, and by the time I arrived in 1980, it was considered by many to be at its peak. Renowned as *the* after-hours club, they were open until 6:00 a.m. on

Saturdays, so it was the place to be when all other clubs shut their doors promptly at 2:00 a.m. The famous cluster of mirror balls that hung above the large dance floor was a sight to behold. It was spellbinding to watch each ball as it constantly spun and reflected beams of light from all directions. The beams poured across the room, and it seemed as though they were a source of energy for the dancers below. As the night would wind down, I'd go upstairs to the balcony and take in the view—a sea of men swaying in unison. I went to the Trocadero for the music, and I also went to dance and simply be with friends.

For me, disco was not music by The Bee Gees or KC and the Sunshine Band. The music I loved was by Donna Summer, Voyage, and Sylvester. I even loved the less mainstream Village People songs; "San Francisco (You've Got Me)" was one of my favorites. The lyrics best describe this time and place that was unlike any other.

> *Fulsom [sic] street [sic] on the way to*
> *...Polk and Castro you know by night by night*
> *Freedom is in the air, yeah*
> *...searching for what we all treasure, pleasure*
> *...Cycles in the night, shining bright*
> *...bright neon lights tell the glory, story*
> *Leather, leather, leather baby*
> *...levi's and keys on the left now or right*
>
> *Dress the way you please and put your mind at ease*
> *It's a city known for it's [sic] freedom...*
> *Cycles shining bright, break the silence of the night*
> *Inhibitions, no, you don't need them...*
>
> *...San Francisco, City by the Bay...*
> *...San Francisco... You've got me*

Dressed for an evening out at the Trocadero. The photo was taken by Eugene in his makeshift studio at home in the Marina. 1983.

The sound of the dancers' heavy boots as they stomped the parquet floor, along with the sound of their whistles and tambourines, only added to the music, as though they worked in unison to create a symphony. The dance floor was usually packed with men dressed only in jock straps, leather chaps and caps, or jeans. My cousin Rebecca, who also lived in San Francisco for a time, was frequently with me at the Trocadero. There we'd be—among the men—dressed to the nines in our Saint Laurent and stiletto heels, utterly rapt in the music. Thick with the smell of poppers or amyl nitrate—a liquid stimulant— the air hung heavily in the room, creating yet another distinctive layer of the Trocadero experience.

CHAPTER NINE

A Dose of Reality

As planned, I joined my sisters at the University of San Francisco, a private Jesuit college, in the fall of 1980. In my first semester, I was surprisingly excited about this new phase in life and did quite well—my grade point average was 3.6. With each passing year, however, I became less motivated and my absences steadily increased, which was no wonder since there was a lot going on in my life at that time. In addition to focusing on a busy social life, my family was going through a major upheaval.

Daddy retired when we moved to San Francisco, so from that point on our family had no means of support. Yet there weren't any changes in our lifestyle. Our lives remained, on the surface, as they had always been with the private schools and the shopping sprees.

I do not recall when I first began to understand the gravity of our financial situation, but the signs had been there for quite some time. When was it that my parents began meeting in the dining room, discussing things in hushed voices during the late hours? And when was it that I had last seen Daddy's smile? His once calm and jovial demeanor had long since disappeared. He even started smoking again after giving up a lifelong addiction only a few years before. He'd light one cigarette after another, completely oblivious to the overflowing ashtray and the ashes scattered about. I never once questioned what was really happening since I was certain this matter—or this inconvenience, as I chose to see it—would eventually pass.

In my view, financial stress was one of those things my mother would take care of, just as she had controlled every other aspect of our lives. On the one hand, she tried her best to deal with what was happening on a practical level by budgeting; on the other was her wish to continue loving us the best way she knew how: by giving us (me) whatever we (I) wanted. For the first several years after I realized we were in financial trouble, our lives continued as they had always been.

"Didn't I tell you not to use your credit card?" my mother asked me outright one day. She was seated at the dining table and held in her hand the credit card statement she'd just received in the mail.

"Yeah, you did."

She looked at the statement through her reading glasses and tilted her head back slightly, as if to sharpen her focus. She demanded, "What, exactly, did you buy for four hundred dollars?"

"A sweater," I answered matter-of-factly.

My mother glared at me above the rim of her reading glasses with pursed lips, then took a deep breath, which seemed to soften her gaze. I sensed she was holding back on what she really wanted to say at that moment and instead commanded, "Stop using that card of yours!" After she placed the statement atop the pile of bills laid out before her, she pulled her checkbook from her purse. This was her cue that I was excused and thus free to leave the room.

During these confrontations, she never once explained why things had to change, so it was easier for me to write off her complaints as a way of simply being hard on me. Even if she had been upfront and said "we can't afford this" or "return that credit card to me *now*," I doubt it would have made much of a difference; I didn't want to hear the unspeakable truth.

In reality, things were terrible and would continue to deteriorate with each passing year. By the time I graduated from college, we'd lost the three family homes in the Marina District as well as our homes on Guam. After years of ignoring the signs, my family's lifestyle had finally come to an end.

Losing the Marina nearly destroyed my mother because it was, without a doubt, the last vestige of Papa's legacy. Not surprisingly, she held onto it for as long as she could, forsaking all else before giving it up. As we busily packed our belongings, I'd find her teary-eyed, muttering intermittently, "Papa loved this house." Reluctant even until the very end, she remained there with Daddy until the morning we were to vacate the premises.

Once my older sisters married and Mama moved in with Uncle, my parents, my three younger siblings, and I moved to the East Bay to begin a new life in a rented three-bedroom condominium. Our move from the Marina was when reality hit hard. When I looked out our windows, I no longer had a sweeping view of the Bay. Instead, I looked directly into a neighbor's apartment. With a total of six individuals (more specifically, six adults) living in tight quarters, tempers frequently flared and the cold silences that followed made everything seem even more overwhelming. I had an especially difficult time dealing with my parents, frequently snapping at them without just cause. For years, I blamed my mother in particular for losing what I had taken for granted all my life: our financial security. As for my father, I resented his inability to exert himself, even during our family's most desperate time. Simply put, I felt my siblings and I had been set up. Self-reliance had not been instilled in us, and then, suddenly, we were on our own.

It took years before I could even understand the value of the experience. In many ways, it was probably the best thing that could have happened to my younger siblings and me; once our family's wealth disappeared, we quickly learned the value of hard work and money. The other good that came out of this experience was that it brought my relationship with Genny and Eugene to another level. (Glenn was still in his teens at that point and therefore was not as aware or affected.) We turned to one another for support, thus creating an even deeper bond among the three of us that no one else could ever understand, not even our older sisters; they, too, weren't fully aware of the tremendous pressures we felt having to remain at home with our parents, who now needed us as much as we needed them.

Matters were made worse by the fact that our only means of support was what little money the family had in its accounts. No matter how desperate our situation grew, our parents never suggested to us that we should begin working. It was only when I could no longer go shopping and when I had less pocket money that I (as well as the others) decided to get a job. However, I faced some challenges from the onset. I had no prior work experience and I wasn't interested in psychology, which was my area of study. I had, in fact, waited until the very last moment—late in my sophomore year—to declare my major. I had given it little thought when I decided to join Jasmine, who was a few years ahead of me, in the School of Psychology. She and I always had a knack for listening to and supporting people in their time of need, so it seemed like the only viable option for me.

The first job I took, at the age of twenty-four, was as a receptionist for a travel firm in downtown San Francisco. Besides the travel perks that came along with the job, I genuinely enjoyed the work and liked the idea of earning my own money. Although most of us hadn't begun working until our early twenties, we were diligent and excelled in what we did. After two years with the firm, I was promoted to a management position. I was, indeed, adapting to my new life and would continue to do so in the years that followed.

Living on a budget eventually became almost second nature. I would consistently allocate my salary towards my share of household expenses and put some into a savings account each month. And still, I always had enough money left for clothes and shoes. My classic sense of style also worked to my advantage since I could wear many of the clothes I had bought in the past without looking dated. Because of this, I was able to keep up with at least some of the illusions in my life. Outwardly, it appeared as though my life hadn't changed. Although I was slowly adapting, I was still pretending that things were as I thought they should have been.

Hiding the truth about my family's financial situation from my close friends was yet another way of pretending for me. Not talking about the harsh realities somehow made them less real. I never had any problems joking about our financial troubles, however. I once explained that we moved from the Marina to a much smaller home with a simple quip: "Oh, yeah. We had to move from the Marina because the traffic there was getting to be a *real* nightmare." Sensing my discomfort, perhaps, or simply out of the goodness of their hearts, my friends mercifully failed to confront me about the truth.

CHAPTER TEN

First Love

Other than my cadre of gay pals, my closest friends in school and afterwards were all from Iran. The Iranian Revolution in the late 1970s resulted in the mass migration of Iranians to the United States. Iranians were, therefore, one of the largest minority groups on campus when I began college in 1980.

Jasmine and Joyce were both engaged to Iranian men, and I was subsequently introduced to the culture through their ties. Both I and my sisters related more closely to these men than to most of the "Americans" we met at school because their culture was similar to our own isolated, family-centric Chinese upbringing. They, too, maintained traditional, solid family values that came before much of what typical Americans thought important. In a way, it was refreshing to meet peers who understood why I continued to live with family and that, unlike my brothers, my sisters and I were expected to remain at home until we eventually married—ideas that were so firmly rooted in my subconscious that I hardly gave them much thought.

In addition to cultural knowledge and expansion, my friendship with Iranians introduced me to the more artistic side of their culture. I gained a genuine appreciation of Iranian music and cuisine through our frequent interactions, and I had a knack for pronouncing their names as though I were speaking my native tongue. I learned quickly, for example, the proper use of the long "A" sound. (One of the basics I learned from my circle of friends is that "Iranian" is pronounced ee-RAH-nian, not ee-RAY-nian.) In time, my family and I adopted Iranian customs as well. For instance, we would kiss both cheeks upon greeting our Iranian friends and even, on occasion, one another. Not surprisingly, it wasn't long before I became completely assimilated into their culture.

In preparation for their impending nuptials, my sisters learned the art of Persian cooking and were constantly testing recipes at home. Many of the dishes quickly became family favorites. Even today, our table is lined up with a unique blend of Chinese, Filipino, Chamorro, and Persian dishes during family gatherings and holidays. As my sisters mastered the art of Persian cooking during those early years, the aroma of flavors such as parsley, lime, cinnamon, and saffron would often waft from our kitchen. This awakened my senses on yet another level, thus completing my assimilation into a culture that was equally, in many ways, different from my own.

I was both baffled and intrigued by Iranian people, particularly those who were from traditional backgrounds where women are considered subservient to men. Growing up with my mother's domineering ways, this contradictory idea of a strong male and subservient female appealed to me in a way.

"Why don't you wear my black cashmere sweater with your new skirt," I said to Joyce one night as we were dressing to go out for dinner with the family.

"You know *he* doesn't like it when I wear V-neck sweaters because it cuts too low in front," my sister replied as she reached for the buttons on her shirt, as if to ensure it was buttoned all the way to the top, just as her boyfriend preferred.

"Oh, that!" I responded, "Well, he's not joining us tonight, so what difference would it make?"

"Oh no, I can't do that," my sister said as she shook her head and her eyes fell downcast.

"Well, suit yourself, but I think it would make a great outfit!"

Her boyfriend's control was very much like the control our mother exerted over us—because we were her children and she loved us. Admittedly, when I saw men treat women in this manner, I thus interpreted it as "love." Therefore, it was no surprise that, at age twenty-two, my first serious romance would be with an Iranian man.

Introduced by mutual friends, Ali and I began dating during my senior year in college. He was twenty-six and worked as a civil engineer, temporarily assigned in the city for a few months. Since emigrating in his early teens, Ali had been living just outside the city, in San Jose.

Ali hailed from Northern Iran—along the Caspian Sea— and like most from that region, he had much lighter features: fair skin with light brown hair and hazel green eyes. In this respect, he did not appease my preference for men with Mediterranean features: olive complexion, dark hair, and dark eyes. Additionally, I wasn't attracted to many of Ali's random traits, such as his nervous habit of chuckling. He seemed unsure of himself and intimidated by me to such a degree that his hands would tremble when lighting my cigarette, disappointing me in my search for a strong male in my life. He wasn't at all the bold and sophisticated suitor I'd been hoping for.

It was time itself that made Ali more attractive in my eyes— there was a gentleness about him that I found difficult to resist. For instance, it wasn't long before I began seeing his once-annoying nervous demeanor as a reflection of deep sensitivity.

Again, without much conscious thought on the matter, I found myself getting not what I had wanted (a domineering man to stand in as my mother) but what I needed (a soft, sensitive soul who understood the complexities of my culture).

For the first several months of our courtship, my mother was completely unaware of my relationship with Ali. However, by the time his job in the city had ended, I knew that I wanted to continue seeing him. Of course, this meant my mother had to be informed. Our relationship was getting serious, and Ali had been uncomfortable with the secrecy from the very start.

"I'll be waiting for you at my garage at 7:00 tonight, so just park your car a couple of houses away and I'll walk over to meet you," I instructed Ali over the phone one Friday morning.

"I don't understand why you just can't tell your mother we're seeing each other," Ali gently said. "It would make things so much easier."

"I just can't; you don't know her."

However, a part of me was growing tired of the game my mother and I had played over the years, of pretending I was someone I was not. I wanted to lead the life of a more normal young woman—one who was involved in a relationship. Lying to her took both energy and patience, which I no longer had.

In retrospect, my desire to take things to the next level with Ali may well have been part of an unconscious effort to abandon my childish romantic notions and ideals. For years, I had steadfastly believed in the storybook romance—I thought I would *know* the moment I met "the one." There would be no need for secrets or "growing" on one another. At the age of twenty-two, I was still waiting for that special someone who'd make my heart flutter or make me feel any of the other signs of being in love, and Ali didn't provide that—at least not in the "happily ever after" romantic sense. However, I liked him, I respected him, and I wanted to be in a relationship with him and, at that point, that was enough.

I had never seen this storybook ending come to pass, nor had I heard of it taking place among anyone I knew. I figured there was truth to the idea of learning to love someone, and whom better than Ali to test this theory with? He was perfect in every other way.

And so about five months into our relationship, I invited Ali to my twenty-third birthday party, which I held at the Marina a few years before my family sold it. I never informed him of my decision to reveal the secret but simply asked him to attend. He, in turn, never questioned my intentions. It was as if we both knew it was time to take the relationship to the next level. Inseparable throughout the night, we danced only with each other.

Although I had introduced him to my parents earlier in the evening, my mother later casually asked, "So, who is that guy?"

I replied, "Oh, he's a friend from school."

The morning after the party, I told my mother I was going out for lunch.

"All right," she said. "Do you need money?" This was before I had started my job.

"No, actually," I said. "My friend, the one you met last night, is taking me out."

She quickly shook the pot of boiling water and eggs and lowered the heat, then turned to me and smiled. "I knew there was something going on," she said. "He seems nice. You can go, but don't come home too late, okay?"

"Yeah," I obediently replied. "I won't be home late." It was as if we were both still giving her the sense of control she no longer had.

I walked away in disbelief. If I'd had known it was going to be that easy, I would have long ago revealed this part of my life to my mother. Elated, I ran upstairs to get dressed for our date.

Ali did all the right things, like frequently giving me presents and flowers, driving for our dates, and paying for all expenses. In addition, he would mail notes during the week telling me how much he missed and loved me. When I wrote about him in my journal, the phrase that came up time and time again was "my wonderful Ali." It's no surprise that my mother became just as enthralled as I was by his efforts and devotion.

Although my mother quickly accepted our relationship, I was still expected to come home every night. Therefore, for the next four years, Ali's hour-long commute each weekend typically began on a Friday night and ended on Sunday evening. He would drive to the city after work and we would have a full evening, going out for dinner and sometimes dancing. Afterwards, he would stay with his relatives who lived just outside the city. Years later, he confessed that there were many nights he was so exhausted that he would park his car around the corner from my house and sleep there until our date the next morning. Our Saturdays and Sundays consisted mostly of outings in the city—museums, the cinema, or shopping on Union Square.

The very first time we danced was to Tony Bennett's "I Left My Heart in San Francisco." I had always thought of the song as old-fashioned music belonging to my mother's generation. But that night, at a nightspot atop the Saint Francis Hotel, as Ali held me closely on the crowded dancefloor, we relaxed into each other's arms. For the first time, I appreciated the sound of Bennett's voice along with the beautiful lyrics and melody.

Like my parents before me, this period in my life would be forever referred to as "the time I fell in love," but it was not just Ali who stole my heart. In many ways, falling in love renewed my passion for San Francisco itself—the passion I'd first felt when I lived in the city after Papa's death. I was finally experiencing the city I already loved in the way it had always been renowned. San Francisco was my true first love, after all, and as I saw it through the eyes of someone in love, each of the qualities I'd always cherished about the city grew more dear and sacred to my heart. Even the familiar sound of the cable car bells suddenly evoked romance.

Unfortunately, the reality of our living situation was still a challenge. Even though he called every weeknight, it was hard to be apart from Ali so much. Our partings each Sunday became a continual loss, one that repeated week after week, leaving me mentally and physically exhausted. Throughout the day, we clung to one another by holding hands and hugging, acting as if it would somehow delay the evening's inevitable goodbyes. I worried about him on his long drive home, especially when he departed late. No matter what hour of the night he left, I would wait up for the call confirming his safe arrival home.

Then came a critical point in our relationship when we saw each other even less. In addition to his full-time job, Ali had become a partner in a successful development company that specialized in building upscale homes in the South Bay. Unfortunately, this required weekend work in San Jose. He tried to compromise by scheduling his on-site shifts for every other weekend, but this only exacerbated our now biweekly partings.

This is not to say I spent my weekdays pining for Ali. Despite my sadness over our separation, I always saw the advantages to our situation since it made us appreciate the times we were together much more than if we saw each other daily. We enjoyed dinners in the city, movies, concerts, or day-long drives along the Pacific Coast (always ensuring that

I was home at a decent hour) because they weren't an everyday occurrence.

Looking back, however, I wonder if the novelty-like nature of our time together impacted my view of our relationship. Was our limited time together the reason that our relationship was so peaceful and loving? We were so different that perhaps things shouldn't have been as smooth as they were. Yet the idea of two complementary personalities coming together and living peacefully wasn't so far-fetched. I only had to look back at my parents' relationship (which made our home tick reliably, like an old clock) to know it was possible.

I first saw a solid future with Ali during a family gathering at his cousin Affi's home. "Everyone, please continue with dinner and I'll figure out what the little one needs," Affi said as her newborn cried during the meal. "I'm not sure why she's being so fussy since I just fed her, and her diaper is dry."

Ali stood up from his seat beside me at the dining table and headed towards Affi. "No, no," he said. "Give her to me. You've been cooking all day, so you have a seat and I'll see if I can get her to stop crying." He took the baby into his arms and began speaking to her in Farsi. "Hey, beautiful girl," he said. "What are you crying about, huh?" He cradled her and swayed from side to side as he stood by the bassinet. Within minutes, the crying stopped.

"Ali is so good with children," Affi said, and everyone murmured in agreement. Both Affi and Ali's mother looked at me and smiled. Ali then looked at me from across the table and gave me a knowing wink, the one that meant, "We'll be having babies of our own someday." I grinned cheerfully and, as always, was impressed by Ali's amazing ability to connect with children. Although I loved kids, I wasn't a natural with them.

*At a dress fitting in downtown San Francisco, in preparation
for my September wedding. March 1988.*

For example, I'd hold an infant in my arms only if I was seated, for fear of dropping the baby.

Soon, after many of my cousins had married and begun their own families, I became obsessed with the prospect of eventually having a family of my own. Ali was right on board with me on that regard. It didn't take long before I became a "squealer," squealing in delight each time I encountered children. Buying presents for my nieces and nephews became a favorite pastime, not only out of my adoration for them but to also give me an excuse to browse through baby shops and fantasize about how I would soon be shopping for my own children.

Then, the birth of my sister Joyce's daughter, Yasaman—the first child in our immediate family—brought this love for children to yet another level. Yasi became a surrogate daughter to me. She was the child I longed for. Besides taking her out at least once a week, I showered her with toys and clothes. I brought her a surprise, no matter how small, each time I saw her. When I began working and received my first paycheck, one of the first things I did was to take two-year-old Yasi on a shopping spree.

"I want that one," Yasi exclaimed while safely nestled in front of me in a shopping cart. She pointed to a small blue ball on the store shelf.

"No, Yasi, we can't get that because you already chose the red one," I reminded her as I reached for the red ball in the back of the cart. "You see, you already have a ball. So, which one do you want—this red one or the blue one?"

Her furrowed brows aligned with her short bangs, and Yasi held the tip of her finger underneath her front teeth, deep in thought. She finally said, "That one!" and pointed to the red ball I held in front of her.

"Here, why don't you hold on to it? We'll see what else we can find in the other aisles."

Yasi cupped the ball with both hands, looked at me with a grin so wide it brought out the dimples on both sides of her mouth, and said, "For me?!" By the time we left the store, we had a cart full of toys.

In 1987, just after the 50th Anniversary celebration of the Golden Gate Bridge, Ali and I set out early one morning to hike on a trail that ran alongside the grand monument. Ali held out his hand with each step as we made our way down the sloping trail; he stayed one step ahead of me at all times to ensure the chosen path was safe. When we reached the very bottom, there was a sweeping view of the Golden Gate Bridge in all its magnificence. The gleaming blue sky was a perfect backdrop for the orange-red structure. The late morning sun beat down onto the heavily wooded trail, and just then, Ali turned and wrapped his arms around my waist. I stood on a slope that was on slightly higher ground, and he gently brought me down to stand beside him. As we laughed and held each other, my head tilted back slightly and I caught a glimpse of the canopy of leaves just above us with the sunlight filtering through. The moment was perfect—one that I needed to remember.

PART TWO

A TIME OF SUDDEN
CATASTROPHIC EVENTS

CHAPTER ELEVEN

The Thunderclap: April 17, 1988

The fever began in the first week of April, on Sizdah Be-Dar. Thirteen days after their New Year, which is on the spring equinox, Iranians commemorate the day by picnicking outdoors. That year, Ali's family attended a community gathering held at a park in San Jose. My sister Joyce, her husband, and Yasi also joined us for the day's festivities.

When I awoke that morning, I had a slight fever and was certain I'd caught a virus. Yet despite my poor condition, I got up and dressed for the day, as always. With full makeup in place, I donned my favorite linen pants along with a cotton sweater set, jacket, and black ballet flats. By the time we arrived at the park, I was feverish to the point where my body ached—a kind of ache that was so widespread it hurt just brushing my fingers through my hair. I wondered how I could have come down with such a bad virus when all around me it was spring. The birds' songs and the brilliant blue sky didn't at all reflect the way I felt.

It was a sunny and warm day, but I shivered throughout the celebration despite having Ali's heavy leather jacket draped across my shoulders, over my own heavy jacket. For added warmth, I used my shoulder-length hair to cover my neck underneath Ali's jacket. The fever chills made me feel as though it were the dead of winter.

During lunch, I could only pick at my plateful of saffron

buttered rice, grilled tomatoes, and kabob, a dish I normally would have finished in no time at all. In the back of my mind, I was grateful for the timeliness of this ailment since it would surely help in my goal of losing a few more pounds before the wedding, which was now only five months away.

At one point in the day, Ali's cousin invited me to join her in the ritual of "tying grass"—*sabzeh gereh zadan*—which literally entails tying two blades of grass together and making a wish. This tradition is normally reserved for single young women who are hoping to marry within the New Year, or at least in the near future. After I explained that I felt too ill to partake in it, she said that it didn't matter anyhow since my wedding was fast approaching.

I didn't want to spoil Ali's day so I didn't tell him, or anyone else for that matter, just how badly I felt. Early in the day, I even mustered the strength to take four-year-old Yasi to the playground. A shy and timid child, she agreed to join the other kids if I held her hand as she carefully walked up the slide, but once on top, she began to cry as a rowdy group of boys yelled and pushed one another. "Don't be afraid. I'm right here," I assured Yasi with my arms outstretched. "Come on! I'll catch you at the other end!"

My words were to no avail, so we instead spent our time walking barefoot on the playground's warm sand. Later, Ali came by and took our picture. We stood beside one another and I looked down at her, beaming. In the photo, I hold our shoes in one hand; with the other, I clutch Yasi's hand almost as tightly as she clutches mine. Whenever I look at this picture, I'm astonished at how well I hid my agony beneath a smile.

When I took my temperature at home that evening, it was 104 degrees.

"Doctors" had never played a role in my family's life, and I

Yasi and me at the park that fateful spring day. April 1988.

guess we'd been lucky over the years that our ailments were easily remedied at home. Besides, wasn't seeking medical attention only required in dire circumstances? I wasn't sure exactly what would call for such measures, but I didn't think I was that sick. I was, after all, still walking and breathing, so in my mind, it was highly unlikely that my condition was serious. Unbelievably, a full week would pass before I sought medical attention, arriving at this decision only after my mother's prescription of chicken soup, Tylenol, and bed rest had failed to alleviate my high temperature.

An aunt recommended a physician who, as I'd later learn, was more of an acquaintance. At my appointment, I informed the doctor of my high temperature, which had remained constant for a week, and I also mentioned the boil that had appeared on my leg a few days after the fever began. I haplessly failed to mention the mysterious bruises that had first appeared on my body about a month previously because I thought I'd figured out the cause. One night, I'd awoken and found myself standing by my bedroom window opening the shades. I was sleepwalking, something I hadn't done since childhood.

My notoriety as a sleepwalker had begun when I was nine years old, during my first summer in San Francisco. Early one morning, I awoke and found Papa maneuvering himself around me to get out of his king size bed. "How did Julie get here?" he asked Mama. I was also confused as to how I'd gotten there since the last thing I remembered was falling asleep in my own bed the night before. I pretended I was still asleep, buying me time to understand what had happened.

"I don't know," Mama had answered. "She was there when I woke up. Maybe her mom brought her in." As they would later surmise, I had walked in my sleep from the bedroom I shared with my sisters and headed across the hall to Papa and

Mama's room. I then managed to position myself on the edge
of the bed, next to Papa. When I finally sat up that morning, I
discovered I was at the very edge of the bed and was surprised
I hadn't fallen off during the night. Thus began a series of
sleepwalking episodes that summer that ended several weeks
later as mysteriously as they had begun. For the next few years,
additional episodes occurred sporadically, lasting several weeks
each time.

When the mysterious bruises appeared many years later, I
speculated that I must have started sleepwalking again.
However, this explanation didn't account for the bruises on my
inner arms or legs. I didn't question it, and I didn't wonder why
the episodes would recur over a decade later. What other
explanation for my bruises could there be?

Since I was certain that I had been sleepwalking, I didn't
think there was any reason to mention the bruises when I saw
the doctor. I also failed to mention just how tired and weak I
had been feeling during the previous weeks. Or had it been
months? At some point, it had become increasingly difficult to
keep up with others during physical activity—for instance,
while out walking. Worse still, I'd always fall fast asleep in Ali's
car, even during our short drives to lunch or dinner. But I'd
convinced myself that almost everyone experiences inexplicable
periods of low energy at one time or another, and I was certain
that I would feel better in no time.

After taking my temperature and examining the boil, which
took about ten minutes in all, the doctor concluded without
further investigation that I had a virus. Her prescription of
antibiotics and bed rest confirmed the idea that I was not
seriously ill.

Within a matter of days, though, my symptoms worsened.
I also developed a painful infection in my throat. Consequently,

I could only speak in a soft, hushed tone. It was also unlike any sore throat I had ever experienced. Eating or drinking liquids, whether they were hot, cold, or even at room temperature, became so agonizing that I simply stopped.

At some point, Jasmine called the doctor to inform her of my deteriorating condition. The doctor reiterated that I was getting over a "bad case of the flu" and instructed that I simply continue taking the medication she had prescribed a week earlier.

By then, part of me knew that my illness was getting worse. Tired of the sound of the television blaring in the background, I'd turn it off and lay in bed in total silence.

"Hey Jul," Glenn said as he came in my room one morning. "Since your throat is hurting and you can't raise your voice, I thought this would help." He placed on my bedside table a small brass bell with a wooden handle. "Just ring it if you need us."

"All right, thanks," I responded in a hoarse whisper.

Not knowing any better, I didn't listen to my body and instead believed what the doctor had said. Looking back on it now, I question how I could have been so calm and indifferent about my symptoms: the 104-degree temperature, the angry and persistent boil on my leg, the bruises, and now the excruciating throat infection. These symptoms were so extreme that they frequently brought me to tears. Indeed, this was no ordinary virus. To avoid acknowledging the unthinkable, it seems the human mind can convince itself of almost anything. *This is just a bad case of the flu*, I reminded myself over and over. By Sunday evening, April 17, 1988—two weeks since the fever had begun—red, pinhead-sized bruises appeared throughout my body, particularly concentrated in my arms. And still, I was not alarmed. My sleepwalking theory, along with the doctor's diagnosis, kept me in a state of inaction.

For the previous two weekends, Ali had served as relief for

my mother by taking over my care. That night, he prepared a pot of chicken soup as I sat at the dining table with my head resting on my arms. As the smell of the hearty chicken-and-vegetable broth filled the room, it only seemed to exacerbate my frail condition. I struggled to finish a small bowl.

I had lost about twenty pounds by that time, which further complicated my condition. I was so weak that I could hardly stand, or even sit. Because I hadn't weighed myself or dressed to go out since my illness began, I was unaware of my dramatic weight loss. Ali and my family members also failed to see my emaciated state because they were around me so often.

At around ten that evening, Ali left for his drive home. While awaiting the telephone call confirming his safe arrival home, I lay in bed, on top of the covers, and watched television. I wore the clothes I'd had on all day—black jogging pants, a green T-shirt, and socks. I felt a little better, or at least I convinced myself that I did. I'd had a mild case of cabin fever for a few days and was looking forward to returning to the ordinary things in my life, like work.

I glanced across the room to the large, oblong clock that hung on the wall next to the television and saw that it was 10:30 p.m. The clock had been Ali's Christmas present to me a few years earlier. Because of its size and its position in the room, the clock was always the last thing I saw when I went to bed at night and the first thing I saw in the morning. I realized it wouldn't be long before Ali called. Then suddenly, I felt lightheaded. It was that same feeling I used to get as a child when I would twirl in one spot so I could feel like I was floating.

Although the peculiar sensation lasted only seconds, I knew there was something wrong since it was immediately followed by a strong tingling sensation in my left arm, as though it were asleep. I sat up in bed and tried moving my arm. It was still. Apprehensively, I tried moving it once more, but it remained completely still. With each attempt, I concentrated intensely, but the only part of my body that moved was my left shoulder (and only because my other shoulder had pulled back). Bewildered, I watched in amazement as my left arm dragged behind me on the bed. Not knowing what else to do, I used my other hand to lift my arm by the wrist. I held it out beside me at shoulder height and then released it. My eyes widened when, to my surprise, my limp arm fell on the bed with a heavy "thump." I knew I needed help. My parents were in the living room, but I didn't want to alarm them, especially my mother, who I imagined would be frantic. Instead, I headed to the bedroom next to mine, where Eugene and Genny were watching television.

I walked barefooted into the room with my affected arm dangling by my side. I calmly whispered, "There's something wrong, you guys. I can't move my arm."

"What? What's wrong?" they both responded.

I walked around the room for a minute or so before my left knee buckled and I fell onto the bed in a sitting position, my legs dangling over the side. I immediately fell onto my back so my head was at the center of the bed. Whatever was happening to me, it was also affecting my leg. Eugene got on the bed behind me and pulled me into a reclined position with my feet still on the floor. I wasn't able to sit up on my own. It was at that point that I began to panic.

I cried out as loudly as I could, louder than I'd spoken in days. "What's wrong with me? I'm going to die!" There was a stabbing pain in my throat. Within minutes, the entire left side of my body, from my face to my foot, had become completely paralyzed. Genny picked up the telephone and dialed 9-1-1. She and Eugene tried their best to comfort me by listening to my cries and saying things like "the paramedics will be here soon" and "you're going to be okay."

My mother panicked when she found out what was happening. "What do you mean, you can't move?!"

Eugene and Genny worked as a single unit that night, to such an extent that I can remember the response to my mother's question but I have no idea who actually said the words. "We don't know why she can't move. We've called 9-1-1. An ambulance is on its way."

Perhaps in a desperate attempt to understand the situation, my mother asked question after question—questions to which there were no answers. We worried that if my mother remained in the room, it would make her more nervous, which would, in turn, only heighten our own anxiety. It was, therefore, a relief when someone finally said, "Why don't you and Daddy wait out in the living room for the paramedics so that you can let them in?" This probably helped my mother immensely. I imagine it was a relief for her to see that my siblings had control of the situation and all she had to focus on was her assigned task of directing the paramedics to the bedroom upon their arrival. She complied without question but intermittently checked in as they waited for the ambulance.

Eugene released his hold on me and placed me gently on the bed so that I lay on my back. He scurried into my bedroom to get my sneakers so that I would be "ready" when the ambulance arrived. This decision seemed to pacify the situation even more, perhaps filling a desperate need for a sense of normalcy. I was going out; I therefore had to put on my shoes. Slowly, I began to calm down.

Even so, putting the shoe on my affected foot proved to be a challenge. I was unable to maneuver like I'd been used to.

Therefore, the reverse had to be done: the shoe itself had to be maneuvered around my foot. Eugene knelt on the floor directly in front of me and wrapped his hand firmly around my ankle, lifting my foot off the ground. He used his other hand to carefully maneuver the shoe, one side at a time, until my foot was firmly inside of it. I couldn't see what he was doing, but the countless times I had helped Yasi put on her shoes came to mind. I felt as though I were a child requiring assistance with a basic task.

I remained in the same position once my shoe was on, lying crosswise on the bed with my feet flat on the floor. Incredibly, my sneakers felt like high heels. My left ankle was unable to support itself and flopped awkwardly onto its side, as though it might sprain. Whatever was happening to me clearly involved my mobility and not my sensation.

The left side of my face felt numb and the paralysis made it difficult to enunciate even the most elementary words, particularly those that began with "L" or "R." Although it felt as if my tongue could position itself to make the desired sound, the words did not come out. If I tried to say "leave," what came out instead was "e-eave." There was a heavy emphasis on the second letter since I was desperately trying to succeed. I began to drool soon after the speech problems began. I became irritated as Eugene and Genny took turns wiping the left corner of my mouth. Only then did I realize that I couldn't even feel myself drooling. What was happening to me?

We began to brainstorm the possible causes of my condition. One idea was that I was dehydrated and lacked nourishment so I'd be fine once I was given fluids at a hospital. However, I was annoyed by this idea after a while because I began to sense on some level that whatever was happening to me was much more serious.

A short time later, the front door opened and I heard male voices that were followed by Daddy directing the paramedics to the bedroom.

The medics walked into the room and towered over Genny and Eugene, who immediately stood aside to get out of their way. The medic with a mustache, the one who appeared to be the lead, came to me and asked, "So, what happened exactly?" I spoke softly and did my best to explain my initial symptoms— the tingling sensation in my arm along with my lightheadedness—in an intelligible manner. Eugene and Genny filled in the words I couldn't enunciate.

"Why don't we get you in a comfortable position here?" the medic said. He lifted my feet off the floor and rotated my body lengthwise on the bed so my head rested on a pillow and my feet were at the foot of the bed. He then sat alongside me and lifted my left hand by its wrist. With my thumb facing me, he instructed, "Let's see if you can move your thumb for me." My thumb was motionless, as though it were completely detached from me and belonged to someone else. I was astounded. "I can't do it," I said.

"What about these bruises on your arms? How did you get them?" The medic inquired. I explained that I hadn't a clue as to how I had gotten them. The medic appeared to be unconvinced as he casually glanced over at Eugene, who stood at the foot of the bed. I sensed that he suspected physical abuse. I didn't have the energy to share my sleepwalking theory or even chuckle at the thought of my own brother as an offender. "*Honestly*," I reiterated, my voice firm, "I don't know how I got them."

The medics appeared to be as confused as the rest of us regarding the cause of the paralysis. After determining that I should be taken to a hospital, they concluded that it would be best to hold my neck in a brace—a precautionary measure in case this was a result of a spinal injury. It was close to midnight as I was carried through the corridor and towards our building's elevator on a stretcher.

Che-Che and her husband—who lived only a short distance away—were waiting in the lobby. She explained that they, along with our mother, would follow the ambulance in their car. Genny and Eugene would remain at home to inform Ali and the rest of the family about what had happened, and Daddy would accompany me in the ambulance.

Once I was settled inside and Daddy was seated up front, one of the medics said, "So, which hospital did you have in mind?"

I had heard numerous horror stories about county hospitals over the years, so I was comforted in knowing that I had medical insurance and some options regarding where I'd end up. By now, the paralysis on my face had intensified to such an extent that I was unintelligible. I had lost complete control of my tongue so that I could no longer position it as I attempted to speak. After several tries, I stated my priorities as best as I could: "Anywhere nice and clean." It sounded more like "Ayee-whey ice ah e-een."

"Okay, we'll take you to Alta Bates in Berkeley. It's a private hospital."

I tilted my head as far back against the pillow as I could to see out through the front window that was behind me. I took note of my agility as I effortlessly brought my neck back. So much for the idea of spinal cord involvement, I thought. And yet I wasn't the least bit comforted by this revelation since ruling it out only meant there was something else going on. Whatever caused such a serious symptom as paralysis must be quite serious itself. The ambulance moved slowly, and although

I could see its flashing red light, there was no siren during the ten-minute trip to the hospital. I took that to mean I'd be okay.

As I was wheeled out of the ambulance, I was amazed by the new perspective that came from lying on a stretcher. In no other situation would I have noticed the ceilings and lights, and yet I took it all in as if I had a breathtaking view. One thought kept running through my mind: *This can't really be happening to me.* I was, without a doubt, in a state of shock. I had grown more and more calm since the initial panic when my leg collapsed and I'd thought I was dying. Perhaps one naturally falls into a state of pure, bewildering detachment when there is no time to think or feel.

The emergency room staff was confused by my symptoms. At one point during my initial exam, a nurse carefully felt the lymph nodes under my arms and around my breasts. This immediately brought to mind a scene from the movie *Terms of Endearment*, when Debra Winger's character is examined for breast cancer. *Yeah, right,* I thought. *Maybe this would be a good time to tell the nurse she's wasting her time. Everyone knows something like that could never happen to ME.*

The medical team questioned the initial care I had received from my physician and was appalled that so much time had elapsed since the onset of the fever. Now, after all of my experience with doctors and illness, I realize that anyone presenting with a high temperature for even a couple of days would need to be examined more thoroughly. Had a blood test been ordered by the internist I had seen a couple of weeks before, she would have discovered an elevated white blood cell count along with decreased platelets and red blood cells.

At one point, the ER staff suspected, among other probable causes, meningitis. They called in a specialist. I soon underwent a painful spinal tap and later, after midnight, a CAT scan. I was too weak to keep up with all that was happening. I wanted to be left alone so I could get some sleep, but the medical team's constant prodding and questioning continued through the middle of the night.

As the baffled physicians assessed my condition, I wore Ali's twenty-inch gold chain necklace. It held two pendants; one was a rectangular gold Islamic medallion that bore the Arabic inscription of "Allah" and the other was the 24-karat gold heart-shaped pendant I had given him about two years before. Ali had once casually commented, "These are from the two women in my life: my mother and Julie." I was thrilled to hear him say those words. *He is, indeed, devoted to me*, I thought. Although it was something he always wore, he had placed it around my neck when we said our goodbyes that night. The necklace was my only solace in the emergency room. As I was wheeled from one examining room to the next, I held the pendants tightly.

By five o'clock in the morning, I was admitted to the intensive care unit. I learned that my paralysis resulted from a massive stroke, also known as a brain attack. The cause of the stroke itself, however, had yet to be determined. The doctors shifted their focus to the matter of my abnormal blood count; they'd discovered an increased level of white blood cells and low platelets. The pieces were slowly coming together. There was something going on with my blood. They scheduled a hematology consult for the next morning.

Once my bed was positioned in the ICU, the nurse ensured that I was comfortable before she left the room and closed the door behind her. It was the first time since my admittance the night before that I'd been left alone. As I lay there, I sensed my limp arm by my side and realized that the left side of my body felt much heavier than normal. I could only lie on my back and stare at the ceiling as I listened to the monitor's intermittent beeping, which underscored the penetrating silence that filled the room.

CHAPTER TWELVE

A Defining Silence

Just after dawn, I awoke in the intensive care unit and saw an IV infusion bag with a thin tube hanging from it; the other end had been inserted into the vein on the top of my right hand. It was covered with tape to keep it in place. I quickly averted my eyes from the insertion site. When and how had it been placed? The last thing I remembered was being left alone in the room until I must have passed out completely.

I glanced around. The stark room had a rectangular glass window that looked out on the nurses' station. Otherwise, it contained just the essentials found in most hospital rooms. A tray table at the foot of my bed held a pink plastic pitcher along with a matching cup and a straw. The walls were bare except for a retractable television that hung at the foot of my bed. The television wasn't on, so the screen only reflected the blinds that were drawn across the large outside window.

My body felt different than it had twenty-four hours earlier. The bed sheets felt heavy on my affected foot, seeming to force my toes downward. It was as though something was pinning my foot to the bed and I was feeling its strain. I later learned that this was one symptom of my body's now-flaccid state. As if to further emphasize the difference, I moved my other ankle up and down, relishing that I could use it to control the featherweight sheets.

A succession of piercing rings jolted me from my reverie.

This was the first occasion on which I was confronted by a once-simple task that had become difficult in my new condition. The phone was on a nightstand to my right, a few inches above my head and further than my unaffected hand could comfortably reach. While I would have normally rolled over to reach for the receiver with my left hand, that was now impossible. While remaining on my back, I extended my right arm above my head, carefully maneuvering it toward the nightstand, turning my hand over to lift the receiver. The movement placed a sharp strain on my shoulder when I successfully completed the task after a few attempts.

"Hel-lo?" My answer was weak. My voice cracked, sounding as though I were hearing it for the first time.

"Hi, sweetheart," Ali began. I found it funny that my heart could still jump at the sound of his voice despite all that had happened.

"Ali, I can't move my arm," was all I could say.

"I know, I know honey. I'll be there in a few hours," he said. "Everything is going to be okay." In times when things are beyond our control, there is no greater comfort than hearing someone say the impossible: "Everything is going to be okay."

Although I do not recall Ali's actual arrival during those first critical days, it seemed that he was in the room whenever I woke up, as if he had been standing or sitting by my side the entire time. I was so comforted by his presence that, truly, the unknown didn't matter.

On that first day, my mother convinced Ali to go home with her and Daddy. He was reluctant, but she argued that he could have a warm, home-cooked meal before spending the night with me. He reluctantly agreed. At home that evening, while everyone was talking about the events of the last twenty-four hours, Ali seemed distant, as though his mind was elsewhere.

"He then came into the kitchen," my mother later told me. "Without looking at me, he said, 'I'm sorry, Mrs. Lee, but I can't stay. I'm going back to see Julie.'"

When he returned that night, Ali pointed to a rollaway bed that was positioned right next to mine. "I asked for a bed," he said. "I've taken time off work, so I'll be here for the next few days." He stayed at the hospital around the clock for the rest of the week, sleeping beside me on the rollaway bed.

For the next two days, my room was filled with family as well as friends. There were so many people coming in and out during visiting hours that it was always a relief when the nurses informed them that I needed to get some rest.

Simply put, I was tired—more so than I'd been in the two weeks since the fever began. It was as though the hospital setting finally allowed me to feel as sick as I truly was. After all, a hospital is a place where the top priority is caring for patients, which gave me permission on some level to do nothing but sleep. All I had to do was lie in bed. It was no wonder that the bed quickly became the center of my world. It was where I received visitors, where I ate my meals—why, it was even where I bathed. Everything beyond its confines was of little or no concern to me.

Within days of arriving in the ICU, the nurses implemented the practice of brushing my teeth with baking soda every few hours. Keeping my mouth clean became a priority to prevent further infections because of my low blood count. They rubbed my teeth and gums with the aid of a small sponge at the end of a plastic stick. The taste and grimy feel of baking soda in my mouth was unpleasant, particularly since I felt so ill.

The job of policing this task was assigned to Ali and my family during the daytime, so it seemed that I was constantly nudged and rudely awakened just to have baking soda in my mouth. It always happened the same way. I'd hear a familiar voice calling out from somewhere far away in the darkness. It was especially irritating when they would sing out the words, the second syllable always at a higher pitch than the first. "Ju-lie. Ju-lie, wake up." Nudge. Nudge. Many times, I would lie still with my eyes closed, hoping it would make the perpetrator go away. But no, the efforts persisted until I gave in. Once, I was so irritated that I opened my eyes and pointed at the culprit with what little strength I had left, then quickly pointed at the door. Jasmine laughed and declared, "Oh, my God! She just told you to get out of here!"

During those first critical days, I was so incapacitated that I was in and out of consciousness. Because of this, my memories are only snippets of what happened around me. There were times when I couldn't even open my eyes so I'd just lie there and listen to my friends and relatives speak in hushed tones. "How did she get so thin?" I once heard someone murmur. "How did it get to this point?" Although I didn't recognize the voice, I knew it was a visitor chatting with one of my sisters.

"I know," one of my sisters replied. "We should have done something sooner and taken her to the hospital, but we trusted what her doctor had said."

In other words, this was a situation that clearly had gotten out of control. Although it would have been easier to blame the doctor for the misdiagnosis, I knew the responsibility ultimately fell on me. Only I knew just how badly I had been feeling. So why did I remain silent and not speak up to demand better care?

Like everything else during this time, these thoughts were fleeting. I was too weak to care about anything other than sleeping, and when I was awake, it was only for long enough to learn what was happening in the moment. I didn't have the energy to think, feel, or blame. Besides, there were more urgent matters to attend to as the medical team narrowed in on a diagnosis.

My blood results showed decreased platelets and an elevated white blood count. The medical team confirmed that my numerous infections likely resulted from a compromised immune system, and they recommended further tests for an accurate diagnosis. They did not, however, share their suspicions about the probable diagnosis, and it never occurred to me to ask. I didn't understand what they meant by "tests," and in truth, I didn't care. Ali and my family, however, were given more specific information when the team scheduled a biopsy of my blood to thoroughly examine my cells. Everyone was horrified. Could this be something as serious as cancer?

Although the medical team did its best to keep the medical equipment out of sight during the biopsy (known as a "bone marrow aspiration"), I happened to catch a glimpse of the needle and syringe as the nurse handed them to the physician right before the procedure began. I was on my stomach because blood cells are produced in the bone marrow, and the largest amount of marrow is found in the rear hipbone. The needle looked thicker than the average hypodermic needle— and worse still, it was at least six inches in length. The syringe was equally thick and large, and it reminded me of the tool bakers use to frost cake. I thought, *They're really going to take out that much marrow from me? How long will it take to fill that syringe?* Seeing the instruments was a great source of trepidation, and it probably made the procedure more painful than it might otherwise have been.

As I lay on my stomach in bed, the physician injected local anesthesia to the back of my hipbone, which was an ordeal itself. He warned it would feel like a sting. It did, but it was a sting unlike any other—the pain was so intense that it vacillated between average and extreme for several long seconds. Once the area was numb, a large hypodermic needle was inserted and quickly twisted down into my hipbone to obtain a sample. This put an indescribable amount of pressure against my entire hipbone, forcing my pelvis against the bed.

The pressure was what allowed the needle to advance through the hard outer layer of bone and into the marrow cavity, an image I couldn't shake. I was blown away by the idea that a needle could penetrate bone, one of the body's hardest tissues. Although the needle placement took only about a minute to complete, it was the most distressing part of the procedure.

Two days after I was admitted to the hospital, a couple of doctors arrived in my room, I was told, to discuss the results of the biopsy. It was clear that whatever they were about to tell me was serious. Ali stood by my bed looking as though he'd been crying. I guessed that he already knew what they were about to tell me. My parents and Genny stood on one side of the room with their heads lowered. I assumed they also knew.

The female doctor who had been overseeing my care began by introducing herself as an internist. She spoke loudly and slowly, over-articulating every syllable. This phenomenon, which would occur time and time again over the ensuing months, always made me feel that the speaker wasn't quite sure if my mind had also been affected by the illness.

She placed her hand on mine, then brought her face closer to mine and looked me squarely in the eye. "WE NOW HAVE A DIAG-NO-SIS," she stated. "YOU HAVE LEU-KE-MI-A."

Her face seemed abnormally large and distorted, as though I was looking at her through a fishbowl.

Except for displays next to retail registers soliciting donations, I didn't have much experience with leukemia and knew almost nothing about it. In fact, the only other time I'd heard of it was when a college friend mentioned that his brother had died of the disease. *It's a disease that can kill,* I thought. "What's leukemia?" I asked the doctor. Thus began a long, drawn-out explanation involving red and white blood cells.

More specifically, my diagnosis was Acute Myelogenous Leukemia, or AML. The doctor continued by saying that there was good news and bad news. The good news was that a cure existed, a bone marrow transplant involving chemotherapy and total body irradiation. "However," she quickly added, "the bad news is that one side effect of the high-dose treatments is—sterility."

"YOU WON'T BE A-BLE TO HAVE CHIL-DREN," she stated, carefully rewording what she had just said, as if to ensure I didn't miss this particular point. I pushed my head back against my pillow. In a hoarse whisper, I weakly repeated, "No children." This time there was no confusion as to what I'd just heard, and I was aware of the potential consequences. For one fleeting moment, I grappled with the idea of going through life without children of my own and questioned the impact this would have on my relationship with Ali. It seems to me now that it was the first piece of information I really heard that morning.

All at once there was an incredible stillness. The silence that filled the room made it feel as if the whole world—and even time itself—had stopped. I could see the doctor's mouth moving, but I couldn't hear anything.

I once read that the Titanic survivors spoke of a silence descending after the ship went down. They said it was even more difficult to bear than the cries that had gone on for hours before. Perhaps it is in this silence when the enormity of the unthinkable first hits us, in a place deep within, absorbing the blow so that it can gently resurface later in time.

Augmenting the impact of this silence, the next several minutes remained a blank space in time for me. For a long time, I thought those moments were forever irretrievable. Then, as we recalled the morning of my diagnosis years later, Genny filled in this lapse of memory. "Yeah, that's what happened," she said. "But you missed something important. Right after the doctor said the part about not having kids, both you and Ali had such a strong look of shock on your faces. You then held each other and began to cry." To this day, I have no recollection of that singular moment.

What I *do* recall is the sense of urgency that morning. It was as if I had entered a world where there was no time to think, let alone feel—an eerie reflection of the disease itself. I had an aggressive form of leukemia. To stay one step ahead of it, we had no choice other than to keep up with its fast pace.

Without any time to process the news, I mentally moved on when the internist introduced the other physician. Until then, he had quietly stood by the window. Having heard my concern, I suppose, the internist went on to explain that this doctor, an oncologist, would now take over my care and could address the adverse side effects of treatment.

Dr. Jeffrey Wolf was a slim and distinguished-looking gentleman in his early forties. He had just the right combination of gray intermixed with his black hair. What struck me the most about him was that he looked old enough to be a doctor and yet was young enough to understand any concerns a person my age might have. Regarding the issue of sterility, he promptly began by discussing the option of freezing my eggs. However, he cautioned that in many cases, this procedure hadn't proven to be successful. At any rate, he stressed the importance of initiating treatment as soon as possible.

Although he had been introduced as an oncologist, it was only after Dr. Wolf's elaboration on treatments such as "chemotherapy" and "radiation therapy" that I even realized I had cancer. Curiously, no one mentioned that word during the meeting, as though not saying it out loud would somehow make it less real. On the contrary, it did the opposite. I recognized on some level that life as I knew it would never again be the same.

I was unfamiliar with the treatments Dr. Wolf mentioned, but one of the few things I'd heard about chemotherapy was that it's a painful treatment involving a burning sensation in the veins. (I later learned that this was a misconception.) Even more frightening was the term "bone marrow transplant," since I could only imagine some complicated surgical procedure whereby a donor's marrow would be literally scooped into my bones.

I was relieved when everyone quietly exited the room, leaving me alone with Ali. He was still standing beside my bed when I turned to look at him. I wanted nothing more than for him to hold me. I thought it would help to ease my fear about the dreaded treatments that had quickly become my foremost concern, for the moment at least.

As we reached out to one another, he held me tightly— almost desperately, even lifting my head from the pillow. He began crying. "*Nothing* has changed. I promise you. *Nothing* has changed."

At first, I found his words comforting; they were his way of reassuring me of his love, no doubt. My eyes widened as he said it again and again: "*Nothing* has changed. *Nothing* has changed." I held on to him and listened to his cries. After a while, it sounded as though he was talking to himself—particularly since he didn't notice that I had stopped crying. Worse still, he sounded like he was trying to convince himself of something he did not believe. As he continued consoling himself, something in me crossed over. To my surprise, his words began to take on a different meaning altogether.

Wasn't he in the room when the doctor informed me that I not only had leukemia but a fate seemingly worse than the cancer itself? "YOU WON'T BE A-BLE TO HAVE CHIL-DREN" was what I had been told outright. So how could anyone possibly say that nothing had changed after hearing what I'd just heard?

As he continued to hold me tightly, I stopped holding on to him. I just lay there with my arm around him, my eyes wide as I listened to his cries.

Then, there was another blank space in time—a deep, dark, and all-too-silent sleep, at last.

CHAPTER THIRTEEN

Cancer 101

"You are very fortunate to have been diagnosed at this time," Dr. Wolf said, "because only five years ago, we didn't have a cure for leukemia." He stood beside by my bed when he said this to me in passing as he concluded his routine morning visit. The power of his words—that there was an actual "cure"—went completely by me. Instead, I was bowled over by his choice of words. *Fortunate?* At the time, I didn't feel very lucky, and I couldn't even fathom the positives in my situation. The only thought that went through my mind was, *Why can't I walk?* I therefore simply smiled and nodded in acknowledgment.

Shortly after being admitted to the hospital, I began a crash course in what I liked to call "Cancer 101." I learned early on that blood cells are produced in the bone marrow, and in the case of leukemia, the body produces abnormal white blood cells. This eventually halts the production of normal white cells altogether, which is problematic since white blood cells defend the body against infections by attacking bacteria, viruses, and germs. This is why I had initially presented symptoms of infection, and, of course, the 104-degree temperature.

My proposed treatment was as follows: I would receive chemotherapy within the next few weeks, which would ideally get me into remission (meaning that I would be cancer-free). Once in remission, I would be discharged from the hospital for a short time, only to return for the transplant. I would first undergo high-dose chemotherapy and radiation treatments, which would essentially obliterate my immune system (along with my reproductive system, I might add). Only after completing the treatments would I be able to receive the donated bone marrow, which would essentially replace my unhealthy marrow with healthy marrow so that my body could begin producing normal cells on its own.

What's more, if the initial chemotherapy worked and I achieved remission, the transplant would give me a thirty percent chance of survival. *It's a little like wiping the slate clean and starting over*, I remember thinking. However, if the chemo treatment failed and did not lead to remission, I would be unable to proceed with the transplant; it would be futile to transplant healthy donor cells if there was any likelihood that cancer cells still remained in my body. Cancer cells grow quickly and multiply at an alarming rate, thus halting the production of healthy cells.

To a layperson like me, the process of selecting a bone marrow donor seems complicated, involving blood tests to find what's called an HLA Match. HLA antigens are the proteins on the surface of white blood cells, and it's important for a donor's HLA to be as similar as possible to the patient's. HLA antigens are inherited from both parents, thus siblings are the best donor candidates.

When I was diagnosed, I learned that there was a twenty-five percent chance that any one of my siblings' HLA antigens would be identical to mine. The closer the match of antigens, the greater the chance their donated marrow would "engraft." In other words, the greater the chance my body would perceive the donated marrow as my own and thus not attack it, as it otherwise would with any invading organism. And conversely, the donor's marrow would perceive that it was in its own environment and not attack my body. Once engraftment occurs, the body begins producing healthy blood cells.

My mother was insulted when Dr. Wolf asked routine questions during the HLA Match procedure. "Of course they're all our children," she vehemently confirmed. She was offended by the suggestion that she might be keeping family secrets despite her history of perpetuating silence.

"Mrs. Lee, please understand," explained Dr. Wolf. "We ask this only because it is at this point when family secrets are typically revealed, such as adoption or half-siblings." I imagine my mother sitting in the consultation room along with my father and siblings, her arms and legs crossed in front of her, having to collect herself after hearing this and reminding herself that Dr. Wolf had only me and my family's best interest in mind. If there was silence to break, he wanted my mother to have the chance to break it on her own terms.

Upon verifying that there were no family secrets and all seven of us were, in fact, full brothers and sisters, the search for a donor began in earnest. After obtaining blood samples from my six siblings, preliminary tests revealed that I am truly a middle child. My three older sisters were more than likely HLA matches with each other, while my three younger siblings made up another set of matches. After comparing the results with my own HLA typing, it was determined that my potential match would most likely be found in the first group—among my older sisters. Further tests of their blood samples would provide a detailed account of eight HLA markers in particular. An ideal donor would have to match at least six of my eight markers.

Then, before the matching process was complete, both Jasmine and Joyce learned they were pregnant.

"Oh my God. You should have seen Dr. Wolf's reaction

when we told him the news—he did *not* look happy!" Jasmine said.

My three older sisters stood by my bed as they gave me a detailed account of what had transpired when they'd broken their unexpected news to Dr. Wolf.

"No, really? What happened?" I asked, eager to learn the outcome of their tale. At that moment, it felt like old times. My sisters and I were together, simply chatting and giggling.

Apparently, Dr. Wolf had looked grim as he went on to explain that the pregnancies were not good news. He told my sisters that even if they were a match, their pregnancies would prevent them from undergoing the basic procedure that was required of donors. This was problematic because I couldn't wait nine months for treatment to be initiated.

"How about you?" Dr. Wolf had finally asked as he turned to Che-Che. "Are *you* pregnant?"

"No, not as far as I know," Che-Che had sheepishly replied.

"Then we better hope you're the match," Dr. Wolf had concluded.

"But don't worry," Joyce assured me. "As we explained to Dr. Wolf, both Jasmine and I have decided that if it comes to that, we'll have to make some tough choices."

Despite this unforeseen turn of events, my treatment remained on course: Che-Che, Joyce, and Jasmine were scheduled for further blood sample tests, which would show just how many of their respective eight HLA markers would match mine. For the time being, Jasmine and Joyce could set aside the tough decisions since there was, after all, one player still left in the game. Che-Che was still a strong contender as my match.

At the time, it *was* like a game. It felt as though I were waiting to pick up the next card in the deck, hoping it would match my remaining one. The gravity of the situation—that this was a life-or-death scenario—had clearly not sunk in.

Within days, we received the results. Che-Che was, in fact, my HLA match.

"Congratulations! That's great news!" Sandy, one of the nurses, said.

"Well, with so many siblings, I never doubted for a moment that I would have a match," was my unenthusiastic response. Leukemia became the "easy" part of it all, at least in comparison to my stroke; therefore, I never questioned the outcome of the diagnosis or its course of treatment. The medical team seemed to have all the answers, so in my mind, things would simply fall into place.

"Actually," my nurse said, "I once knew a patient who also had six siblings, but she didn't have a match, so this *is* really great news!" As always, any statements regarding the positives in my situation went completely past me, so I instead smiled and nodded in acknowledgment.

The news that Che-Che was my match brought back memories of a time that I had long forgotten, a time when there was a great silence—and conflict—between Che-Che and me, and we were all aware of the irony of the situation. Eugene put it best: "Well, I guess Che-Che won," he bantered as we all laughed. My childhood adversary was playing a critical role in my survival, but more importantly, in a twist of fate, the bond between us would now go beyond ordinary blood ties.

We were all aware of the irony, except for Che-Che. "What do you mean, we didn't speak? All I remember was that we fought a lot." With an overall agreeable and positive temperament, my sister has never been one to latch on to grudges of any sort. Instead, she has always lived pragmatically

From right, Che-Che and me on a family vacation in Hong Kong. 1978.
I was sixteen years old and she was twenty. We had no idea what lay ahead for us.

in the here and now, which is perhaps the reason she has no recollection of that time.

Armed with the revelation of a matched sibling who wasn't pregnant, and in preparation for the transplant, Dr. Wolf initiated the first phase of treatment, which was to get me into remission. I was scheduled for my first round of chemotherapy in the week ahead, less than a month after my stroke. Before the medical team could proceed with the induction chemotherapy treatment, however, they had to perform a minor surgical procedure to insert a Hickman catheter, a catheter that is placed into a large vein.

They placed it in the upper right-hand side of my chest, into the subclavian vein, in the area below my clavicle towards my right shoulder. Because of the numerous blood tests I'd receive in the upcoming months, and since chemotherapy is administered intravenously, the catheter would prevent the doctors from over-puncturing my veins.

Although the procedure must have been explained to me in detail, it did not register in my mind like many other things during this time. I knew that Ali and the others were looking out for my best interests, and my trust in them was so implicit that I'd quickly agree to anything so I could be left alone to sleep. This was also a way to avoid thinking too deeply about what was happening to me and what the consequences could be. It was much easier to rely on those around me and take in only as much as I had to.

As always, things moved quickly. It seemed as if I had just been informed about the upcoming procedure when, the next thing I knew, I was being wheeled on a gurney to the surgery center. Ali and my family members were gathered in the corridor outside my room, wishing me well. They all looked tired and concerned, including four-year-old Yasi, who was in her father's arms. Yasi called out to me with furrowed brows, prompting her father to lean closer so that she and I could momentarily hold each other's hands. I was so moved to see Ali and everyone there, but as always, the scene slowly faded. In what seemed like a split second later, I found myself in the operating room.

Before I drifted back to sleep, I caught a glimpse of my surroundings. The spacious room looked exactly as it is depicted in movies and on television. The walls were covered from floor to ceiling with mint green tiles, a shade that I liked to call "hospital green." They closely matched the color of the scrubs and surgical caps donned by the medical team, along with their masks and gloves.

The room was filled with the brightest white light I'd ever seen—not a fluorescent blue color, but a pure white light that reflected off the stainless-steel items that were scattered about, including the tray that held a set of sterilized tools. The air was cold, which prompted me to pull even closer the blanket that covered me. The air smelled the way the room looked—it was a distinct disinfectant smell, and it was stronger there than in any other part of the hospital. Along with the sounds of beeping monitors, I heard murmurs from the medical team all around me as they prepared with an unhurried efficiency. Someone gave me a shot and asked me to count backwards from 100. Slurring, I began, "100, 99..."

"Just relax, Juliane," the doctor said. "You're going to fall asleep now." Barely able to keep my eyes open, my last glimpse was of an oxygen mask that came towards me, gently covering my nose and mouth.

When I came to, I was back in my room with Ali and my family members gathered around me. Although the room was dimly lit, I could see the freshly-stitched inch-long incision on the upper right side of my chest where the catheter had been inserted. It emerged from a small puncture wound between my breasts. Protruding from the hole was a three-inch-long tube that would serve as the administration site for medications, nutrients, or blood products; blood would also be drawn from that spot. Although I was groggy, I cringed at the sight of the wound and thought, *What if the tube was accidentally pulled? Would any vital organs come out with it?*

Because of hospital policy, only a small number of visitors were allowed in my room that night, so friends and family members took turns at my bedside while the others waited in the hall. At one point, I awoke and saw my best friend. Sholeh looked scared and her teary eyes spoke volumes. I could only imagine what a sight I must have been: pale and emaciated with an exposed surgical site. As I calmly looked up at my friend, I wished I had the energy to console her and let her know that I was fine, but I was too weak to utter a word. Sholeh soon began to cry. Ali glanced at my sisters, who stood on the opposite side of my bed from him, prompting them to gently lead Sholeh out the room.

In time, I felt better and regained some of my strength— and when I did, I began to contemplate my situation. As soon as I learned that my first phase of treatment, induction chemotherapy, had been scheduled, I began to ask the medical team for information regarding my two primary concerns. My first concern was my long-held belief that chemotherapy would be painful and my veins would burn, which the team assured me was not the case. Second, I was fearful of the treatment's odious side effects of nausea and vomiting, which I later learned are two of the most commonly feared cancer treatment side effects for patients. For me, the very idea of vomiting was repelling. It is an experience, after all, that involves each of the senses: sound, smell, taste, sight, and even touch as vomit rises through the throat.

On the third week of my hospitalization, my chemotherapy treatment began as scheduled, which, to my surprise, wasn't at all invasive. While I lay in bed in my isolation room, a nurse connected a bag full of the chemo solution to my catheter. For about a week, it slowly dripped into my body for an hour or so each day. I distracted myself by watching television or chatting with visitors. I was hooked up to monitors that tracked my blood pressure, heart rate, and other vital signs. The nurse on shift would come into my room from time to time to check the monitors and would simply adjust the rate of the drip as needed.

To my relief, the nausea and vomiting didn't begin until a couple of days into my treatment, and my case was only moderate rather than severe. Early on, my mother shared her proven way of alleviating queasiness: dried Chinese plums, which she brought by the bagful—for me and also for my two pregnant sisters, who were both in their first trimester. "It's what got me through when I had you all, and it's going to help you now," she instructed.

The hospital's antiseptic smell overwhelmed Joyce and Jasmine as soon as they stepped into the lobby, so we'd chat while sucking on the dried plums. I immediately understood how the plums could remedy nausea. Their pungent taste was immediate; it was at once salty, sweet, and tart and had the power to take the mind and body away from any other experience, even chemotherapy-induced nausea.

CHAPTER FOURTEEN

Fall Out

Eugene stood over my bed with his scissors in hand. Because my shoulder-length hair had been in tangled clusters since I arrived at the hospital, I asked him to cut it for me. Genny was also there, but I was too weak to recall the others who surrounded my bed that morning, a couple of other siblings perhaps. Eugene had positioned my hospital bed to a near-sitting position, then carefully placed pillows around my left arm and shoulder to keep my body in place for the task. Both were dressed from head to toe in their signature black attire, and Eugene stood on my left side while Genny stood on my right. He began to brush my hair with his fingers in a light backward motion, then upwards, then back again, envisioning what my cut should look like.

The 1980s San Francisco Punk culture had made a huge impact on my then-teenage siblings, particularly on Eugene's creative side. Among his many artistic talents, he was self-taught in cutting his own hair—as well as Genny's and their friends'—in the shaved, spiked, crew cut style; he'd even given a few mohawks. I was always impressed by his ability to blend the nonconformist look with his keen aesthetic and attention to detail. The lines were clean and well-balanced. In short, like all of Eugene's creations, his haircuts were a work of art.

"Like we talked about before, I think we should just crop it short," Eugene said. "Which, as you said, should make it easier for you when your hair actually starts to fall off."

"Yeah, all right," was my only response. I was simply too exhausted to care. I just wanted to get the task over and done with so I could be left alone to sleep, which remained my number-one priority. Besides, I had complete trust in Eugene's skills.

To accommodate my frail condition, my brother cut the front part of my hair as I lay perfectly still on my back. My head was pressed against the pillow that one of the nurses had covered with a large towel for the occasion. From time to time, he'd ask me to turn my head to each side as needed. "Okay, now pull your head up away from the pillow," he instructed minutes later. He quickly cut the hair on the back of my head. "And now turn to the side." He swiftly ensured that the front portion blended with the back. The fact that he even completed the task was a testament to his skills since I could barely lift my head from the pillow.

For someone who had always taken great pride in my outward appearance, I was surprisingly not devastated about losing my hair, as one might expect. Unlike my sisters, who had thick, coarse hair, I had always struggled with baby-fine hair that had little volume; I was convinced that it would eventually result in thinning hair. Mama and my aunts had even put the notion into my head that if I cut it short or even shaved my head, it would likely come back thicker. I had never been prepared to take such extreme measures, but the far-fetched idea had somehow stuck. Ironically, my medical situation gave me a reason to do something I had always considered.

Days after my haircut, both Genny and Jasmine walked into my room with new hairdos. They, too, had cropped their shoulder-length hair short. This was no small feat on their part—my sisters didn't even like to put their hair up in chignons or ponytails because they thought they looked better with it down. As they walked into my room with the others, they both kept their eyes on the floor, as though they didn't want to call any special attention to themselves. They had made their decisions separately and asked Eugene to cut their hair, which was how they each learned of the other's plans. I didn't have the energy to fully appreciate the many sacrifices that my sisters and the rest of my family made for me at the time, but today I can only remember it all with tears in my eyes.

"Hey, you cut your hair," I noted, almost in a whisper, as they entered my room.

"Yeah," they muttered, smiling, and quickly looked away. Had we made eye contact, they and I, along with everyone else in the room, would have probably been overcome with emotion. It was much easier to rely on our family's practice of remaining silent on such matters than it was to display our feelings.

Within weeks of beginning my induction chemotherapy treatment, my hair began to fall out in clumps. I was told that it could happen at any time, so I'd begun a morning ritual, which was to run my fingers through my cropped hair a few times, from the front of my head all the way down to the nape of my neck. One morning, as I brushed my fingers through my hair from the front to the back of my head, I felt a patch moving along with my hand. There was no pull or tug; it simply fell away like a pile of leaves carried by a gentle breeze. I then brought my hand up to my face and saw the clumps of hair between my fingers. Sandy, one of my favorite nurses, looked at me. "All right," she said. "It looks like it's started."

"I want it shaved off completely and as soon as possible, please," I replied. Early on, I'd informed my family and the medical team of my wishes. Rather than having small patches of hair on my head, I'd decided to first crop it short, which Eugene had already done. Then, when it began to fall out, I told them I'd shave it all off. The last thing I wanted was to see a significant portion of my hair gone, with only a few strands hanging here and there. Stylistically, my one basic rule of thumb had always been to look clean above all else. A completely bald head was a simpler look, and that in itself appealed to me.

The decision to shave my head also stemmed from my control issues. Cutting my hair short, then later shaving it, would allow me to decide exactly when and, to some extent, how much of it I would lose. Such actions were done instinctively and without much thought, but they made me feel less the victim and more the instigator—thus providing me with a sense of empowerment I so desperately needed. At a time when everything in my life was in such turmoil, it was even more critical for me to control the things I could. Shaving my head allowed me, on some level, to reclaim control of my own fate. In the end, this made me stronger and more confident.

A woman's hair symbolizes her femininity and beauty. Many women voluntarily cut their hair to signal independence or freedom, or to exert control during major life events such as a divorce, breakup, or job loss. Haircuts allow women to symbolically leave their feminine side behind and put forth a warrior-like persona, thus letting go of their former life on some level. This act of letting go can then help them to move forward in their journeys when dealing with such losses. I, too, was dealing with a major life event—a loss—and as a way of exerting control of the situation, I could still determine exactly when and how much of my hair I would lose.

But ultimately, I wasn't devastated about losing my hair because I was completely overwhelmed by the stroke and its side effects. Everything else—including my hair—paled in comparison. Everything else was weighed against what I deemed as the most horrific event. *Yes, my relationship with Ali is uncertain, but why can't I walk? Yes, I have to go through a bone marrow transplant, but why can't I walk? And yes, I'll lose my hair, but why can't I walk?*

I'd regained enough strength to sit up on my own in the weeks since Eugene cut my hair, so Sandy had me sit on a chair near my bed as she cropped it to be even shorter. I was at a high risk for infections because of my low white blood cell count, so to reduce the risk of cuts or injury (which would make me more vulnerable to infections), the nurse on duty was assigned the task of cutting the remaining hair on my head so it was as close to my scalp as possible. I was thrilled that Sandy—one of my favorites—was on shift that day.

Unlike Eugene's cut, Sandy's was done without regard to style. Ali, Che-Che, and Genny stood around us, prepared to lend their support. Occasionally, Sandy would mutter, "Well, it looks like this part's ready to go," as she effortlessly pulled away a clump of hair. I kept my head down throughout the haircut and watched the clumps of hair fall onto my lap and accumulate beside me on the floor. Once she was done, I immediately used my hand to feel the surface of my head. It was uneven; there was no hair at all in some places, while what little remained clung to other spots.

Afterwards Ali took his electric shaver (a Christmas present I had given him two years before) and finished the job, leaving me completely bald. I couldn't see Ali since he and the others stood behind me, but I could feel the warmth of his touch as he used one hand to tenderly move my head to the desired position. Ali was quiet, like everyone else in the room, but I did not sense any reluctance or hesitancy on his part. My mind eventually went blank as I closed my eyes and focused on the quiet buzzing sound of the electric shaver, which had a meditative quality that calmed me even more.

When Ali was finished, Sandy exclaimed, "Wow, you have a really nice head!" Everyone murmured in agreement.

"Really? You think so?" I asked incredulously.

"Yeah, and I'm not just saying that to be nice," Sandy went on. "There are some patients who really can't get away with it, but your head is small, round, and symmetrical."

"Yes," Ali concurred as he moved in front of me and caressed the entire surface of my head. "It's beautiful." I looked up at him and we smiled.

Flattered, I immediately thought of the '80s singer Sinead O'Connor, who I always thought looked better without hair than she did with a full head of hair. Perhaps I could also pull it off? I instinctively reframed a consequence of my illness as something that was less threatening—a statement of style, if you will. I didn't ask for a mirror once it was done, and mercifully, no one offered one.

"I don't want to see myself," I declared. "I just need to feel my head."

As I ran my fingers across the surface of my head, I was particularly drawn to a small patch of skin near the base of my skull. I kept returning to this spot simply because I had never felt such soft skin before. I couldn't believe I had a patch of skin as soft as a newborn's. Everyone was silent as I explored my scalp, perhaps afraid of how I might respond. I sensed they were waiting for me to set the tone with my reaction. If I was sad, they would console me as best they could; if I was happy, they'd smile along with me.

In what would be my characteristic way of handling things in the months ahead, I began to tell jokes, which was my way of letting them know that I was okay with this. As I rubbed my head, I quipped, "Well, I guess my hair won't be an issue that I have to deal with for some time."

"That's right," Che-Che said as everyone chuckled.

Although I had been in charge and had remained calm throughout the entire ordeal, I also knew on some level that losing my hair was, in fact, a *very* big deal. I found myself instinctively staying in the moment. To avoid becoming overwhelmed, I took in only as much as I thought I could handle. I was like a cup that was filled to the brim, and seeing my reflection would have been enough to prompt an overflow. On top of everything else I'd gone through, I knew I had to adjust to my hair loss by first accepting it in my mind and then accepting it tactilely by feeling my head. That had been enough.

I avoided my reflection for what felt like a long time. The only mirror in my room was above the bathroom sink, and it was positioned at a slightly downward angle so that it was accessible to patients in wheelchairs. Getting me into and out of the shower each morning entailed passing the mirror as the nurses maneuvered my rollaway chair, and at first, I averted my eyes.

After a few days, I began catching small glimpses of myself as I was wheeled past the mirror. I got my first full glance by focusing my eyes on the mirror's steel frame, which only allowed me to see a peripheral reflection of myself. Since my eyes were focused solely on the frame, I could only see my head out of the corner of my eye. I was clearly bald since I saw flesh but no dark mass of hair, yet I couldn't make out details such as how my bald head looked with my facial features. I knew these oblique glimpses would only lessen the shock when the time came to look at myself directly in the mirror.

During a morning session with Denise, my physical thera-pist, she placed my chair near the foot of my bed, then asked me to stand and take a few steps towards the bed. When I stood, I saw my reflection in a glass window. It was then that I first saw myself from my head down to my upper torso. I was bald and dressed in a blue-and-white checkered hospital gown. My flaccid left arm was so thin that it appeared to be dangling through the sleeve, and I could see the exaggerated drop of my left shoulder since it was still a challenge to hold my left side up when I was in a standing or even a sitting position. I then saw my strong right arm, my hand tightly gripping a quad-cane. *Oh my God*, I thought. *I'm a cancer patient.*

All the small steps I had taken toward acceptance had prepared me for that moment—cropping my hair and then shaving it, feeling the smooth skin on my head, using my fingertips to map the ridges of my skull. I took a deep breath and refocused my attention on the business at hand. "Remember to look straight ahead and keep your head up. Pull your shoulders back and try to put some weight on your left side," Denise instructed.

"Yes, that's it!" she exclaimed as I took a step forward.

CHAPTER FIFTEEN

Going Home

"You are the reason I went to nursing school!" Ann, an early-morning shift nurse, exclaimed after I transferred on my own from the side of my bed to the commode chair, a portable toilet that sat strategically close to my bedside. She was one of the nurses who'd get me up around dawn to, among other things, wash me for breakfast and prepare me for the nurses on the next shift, who would get me out of bed for the day and into the shower.

"That's amazing since you couldn't do that when I last saw you!" Ann's green eyes sparkled, highlighting the freckles on her face and her luxuriant red hair, which was cut in a short pageboy.

I only saw Ann occasionally so her fresh perspective on my improvement made me hopeful. My progress since the stroke had been steady, and it was the small wins that had gotten me to this point. Basic bodily functions, such as urinating, had initially proved to be among the most challenging and humbling experiences. During the first few weeks, I'd had to endure the unpleasant practice of having a bedpan held underneath me as I lay in bed. Later, when I was strong enough to sit on the side of the bed, nurses would place their arms beneath my underarms to hoist me from the bed, holding me up like a ragdoll and then gently placing me on the commode chair. I had come a long way. I often found it challenging to acknowledge the small wins on my own, so feedback like Ann's was critical—a reminder of how far I had come.

"Denise and I have been working hard on this for some time now," I said with a wide grin. I enjoyed my rehab sessions with Denise and found them to be time well spent since she always gave practical advice such as how to complete chair transfers. Denise taught me to bend forward as I sat on the side of the bed, using the weight of my torso, along with my right hand, to lift myself off the bed. I'd stand momentarily, holding the rail that was attached to the side of my hospital bed, then take a step forward and pivot until my back was directly in front of a chair that was positioned by my bedside.

The nurses often displayed kindness and compassion. They were inspiring, reminding me that life—and the world, for that matter—couldn't be so bad when it was full of so many warm and giving individuals. Not surprisingly, I aptly referred to the nurses as "my angels" at some point. In addition to their role as caretakers, they became my confidants, my sounding boards, and my cheerleaders. Nearly all of the nurses were compassionate, and even encounters with unpleasant ones culminated in kindness.

"No, I can't swallow those that way," I informed Linda one day as she handed me a small paper cup. In it were two oval-shaped potassium tablets, the medication I always referred to as "horse pills" because the tablets were quite large, and thus difficult to swallow—especially in their non-coated tablet form.

Linda responded with an immediate, heavy sigh. "So," she said, "what do you need me to do?" Punctuating her clear annoyance with another heavy sigh, she said, "Do you want it *crushed* in your applesauce?"

Short and stocky with blonde, overly permed hair down to her shoulders, Linda had walked into my room that day expressionless, without a smile on her face, just as she appeared on the ID badge pinned to her green scrub top. Although we had never met, she neither established eye contact nor introduced herself. Instead, she immediately began to tidy up my breakfast tray on the roll-away table that was adjacent to my bed and proceeded with the duties of her shift, such as taking my vitals, my blood pressure, and my temperature.

"Yes, please," I replied meekly. "The nurses mash it in applesauce."

Again without eye contact, Linda promptly turned her back towards me and busily prepared my meds on the roll-away table.

Oh my God, who is she and what has she done with my angels? I thought. Even this experience, however, led to an act of caring. On the next occasion when Linda was assigned to me for the day, I casually asked one of my regular nurses, who dropped by to say hello and check in with me, "Is there any way that you can care for me today?"

"Why, Julie?" Sue asked. "What's wrong?"

"Nothing," I answered halfheartedly.

"Julie, what is it?"

"I just don't feel very comfortable with Linda," I declared.

Minutes later, Sue returned and informed me matter-of-factly, "Okay, I've taken care of it. I'm your nurse today."

It was all I had to say. I never saw the unfriendly one again.

I developed a reputation with the nurses as a "pleasant patient" to whom many requested to be assigned. I sincerely liked each one of them and enjoyed their company immensely. There was the charge nurse, Ligaya—whose name means "happiness" in Tagalog—who became fast friends with my mother. Then there was Gretchen, who offered her personal VHS tape collection as a lending library to patients in the isolation rooms, like mine. However, my two favorites were Suzanne and Sandy simply because there was a lot of laughter in my room whenever I was in their care.

Suzanne was the first nurse I met when I was transferred to the oncology ward. My favorite soap opera, *All My Children,* was on TV as we chatted. At some point, Suzanne glanced at the television and then looked at me with a twinkle in her eye. She said, "You know, we have our own soap opera going on here at the hospital—it's called *As Alta Bates Churns,* and Dr. Wolf is *the* head honcho!" In time, I would come to know firsthand the cast of characters at the facility. Suzanne would become one of the protagonists who would make a great impact on my life. As I wrote in a holiday card to her years later, "The best thing about 1988 was finding you as a friend."

Suzanne was in her late thirties and was someone who easily connected with me, Ali, my siblings, and even my parents. Her long, thick blonde hair was waist-length but always pulled up in two braids at the back of her head. Between that, her broad shoulders, and her solid build, Suzanne reminded me of a sturdy Scandinavian woman. Worn and strong from years of caregiving, her hands were replete with lines and misshaped fingers. Her hands, in fact, looked a lot like my mother's hands—hands that I knew I could rely on.

Sandy, on the contrary, was younger. She was in her late twenties, around my age, and also planning her upcoming nuptials. Our topics of conversation ranged from "where to shop for wedding dresses" to "ideas for the best wedding favors." Looking back on it today, Sandy's sincere appreciation of my feedback gave me a sense of normalcy; despite all I was going through, we were just two young women bonding and commiserating on both the joys and challenges of planning a wedding.

About a month into my hospital stay, Suzanne and Sandy (like most of the other staff members) informed me that a critical part of my recovery was to dress in comfortable clothing and spend short periods throughout the day sitting in an orange vinyl armchair by the window in my room. Undoubtedly, this was to give me a sense of accomplishment. However, I had great difficulty with this request, for the idea wearing a jogging outfit and sitting in a chair all day was depressing. It was something invalids did, not young (and healthy) twenty-six-year-olds.

Lying in bed was more comfortable for me because I was used to it by then, so it didn't challenge me in any way. I didn't say this out loud, and I might not have even been consciously aware of it. In retrospect, however, I realize I was so resistant because a new activity—getting dressed and sitting in a chair— would only make my disability more "real." I would be forced into finding a way to accomplish these tasks, which would in turn bring to light the real issue that I was dealing with a physical disability on account of my stroke. Old people or invalids had strokes—not people like me. I was afraid to join their ranks, and I didn't want to accept that my life had changed, so I did everything I could to ignore my new reality.

Consequently, whenever any of the nurses brought up the idea of changing into my clothes for the rest of the day, I explained that it wasn't possible since my family hadn't brought me any.

"I know the nurses have asked you to bring my clothes. But I really don't want to have to change my clothes, so please don't bring them," I instructed Ali, my siblings, and my parents. "Okay?" I suppose I must have pulled at their heartstrings, for no one questioned my request. How could they deny me with all that I was going through?

My compromise was that if I couldn't get out of sitting in the chair, I could at least avoid the clothes. It felt like a victory to me, albeit a small one, and I was willing to make this compromise because I wasn't ready to consider the bigger implications of disability.

Weeks after I began sitting in the chair dressed in my hospital gown, Suzanne and Sandy arrived in my room early one morning and presented me with my official "daytime outfit," which they'd made especially for me. They'd taken a white cotton pillowcase and cut holes in it for my head and arms, and they'd used multicolored glitter to create a design that read, "Julie's T-shirt." I always wore black cotton leggings with my hospital gown, and now I had a top I could put on as well.

After she handed me my new T-shirt, Suzanne facetiously said, "Now, there really isn't any reason why you can't change your clothes and sit on the chair."

"Okay, whatever you say, *Sarge*," I replied. "By the way, I'm calling you 'Sarge' from now on because your tactics are the very same ones used in military camps—there's just no way out of a direct order."

"Works for me!" Suzanne retorted.

From that point on, I complied and spent an hour or so every day sitting by the window in my room. Although their custom T-shirt was a very sweet gesture, I must admit that it did not appeal to my sense of aesthetics and style. In the end, I therefore relented and requested that my family bring my clothes—Sandy and Suzanne's ultimate goal, I'm sure.

Around the same time that I resisted getting dressed, about a month after my stroke, I began to regain some mobility. The first movement I regained was the ability to lift my affected leg straight up while lying on my back. The neurologist was examining me and Ali was in the room when it happened. After having already failed several of the doctor's requests, ranging from opening my clenched fist to wiggling my toes, I became discouraged. Ali, who was standing at the foot of the bed beside the doctor, appeared to be feeling the same. As the examination proceeded, his head lowered with each of my failed attempts. The physician then instructed me to lift my leg straight up off the bed. *Now that I can do*, I thought, and I proceeded with the task. Though my leg was barely an inch off the bed, I, of course, felt that I had just performed a major feat. In his excitement, Ali brought his hands together in one loud clap and exclaimed an exalted, "Yes!"

As if wanting to bring us back to reality, the doctor quickly noted that my newly regained ability appeared to be coming from my hip, which apparently is not the body part that's normally used when making such a movement. Whether or not it came from my hip was of little concern to me. Couldn't he see that this was *big*, simply because it was something I couldn't do only minutes before? Although the neurologist wasn't impressed with this victory, I was. It pushed me to keep trying despite my mounting frustration, and it gave Ali hope, too.

A few weeks later I took my first step. "Okay," Denise said. "Keep your head up and look straight ahead. I know you can't do this, but I want you to imagine yourself lifting your knee as you take that step forward." Although her instruction registered in my mind, my hip took over and lifted my leg nevertheless. Since I didn't have the ability to lift my knee, I instead used my hip to move forward; therefore, my leg swung out to the side as I took my first step. In the end, it was my hip that enabled me to bring my leg forward—a movement the neurologist had dismissed just weeks earlier. It was an unnatural way to take a step, but it was a step forward nonetheless. I was thrilled.

Shortly thereafter, I learned that I'd soon be released from the hospital because the chemo had worked and I'd gone into remission. I'd be at home for a month to continue my recovery before being readmitted for the bone marrow transplant. I was elated—the idea of sleeping in my own bed, eating my mother's home-cooked meals, and sitting in my own chair to stare out my own window was bliss. It's surprising how much these little things can mean when they're unexpectedly taken away.

"I know you'll be released in a few weeks," the female oncologist said. "I want you to know that for many patients, their first time home can be the most difficult." She was on rounds, checking in with Dr. Wolf's patients because he was out for the day. It wasn't the first time I'd heard this from the medical team. I knew what she was saying, but I couldn't really *understand* it. It was unthinkable to me that being in a comfortable environment, surrounded by my own things, not having to breathe the disinfectant hospital smell, could be challenging.

"Yes," I said. "I understand that returning home can be tough, but I also know I need a break from all this. There's nothing more that I want or need than to be home right now."

Weeks later, two months after my stroke, I left the hospital for the first time. "Why don't I set you down right here so you'll have a clear view of your room and you can see how hard your family is working to gather your things," Suzanne said as she maneuvered my wheelchair to the area in the hallway just outside of my room.

During my two-month hospital stay, I'd only left my room when I was transported on occasion to the physical therapy rehab room down the hall, to the operating room, or to another floor for tests. Since I was typically wheeled either in a chair or on a gurney, I was transported quickly to my destination. There hadn't been much time to soak in the layout of the area just outside my room, or the layout of the rest of the hospital, for that matter. Like in most facilities, the patient rooms were on the periphery of the floor. In sharp contrast to my sunny, cheerful room, there wasn't any natural light in the hallway. Instead, the area was suffused with fluorescent lighting that gave it a cold, institutional feel. However, the medical team's warmth quickly remedied the scene. I was thrilled to simply observe them as they went about their daily tasks.

To provide me with a proper send-off, Suzanne and Sandy had coordinated their work schedules to make sure at least one of them was on shift when I left. In the end, Suzanne was the one who saw me off. She smiled tenderly as she straightened the collar of my blouse. "Okay," she said, positioning me outside of my room. "I'll be back in a bit." Then she hurried off.

She, Sandy, and the rest of the medical team were aware of how much this day meant to me. After two long months in the hospital, I was finally doing the one thing I had dreamed of. I was going home, albeit temporarily. Home was a place where I could be myself and forget that I was a stroke victim, a cancer patient. I looked forward to feeling more normal and not being constantly reminded of my disabilities.

"Hey, you're going home today," a nurse exclaimed as he walked past, punctuating his greeting with a thumbs-up. Donning their white coats, medical charts in hand, doctors walked briskly past me. Many smiled and appeared to share the excitement I was feeling, knowing it was my big day.

I glanced back at my room as Suzanne pushed a cart inside. Ali was unable to take time off work to be there that morning, although he planned to celebrate with us at home later that night. Therefore, it fell to a number of my siblings to dismantle the things that had made the room my very own for two months. They removed the get-well cards that were tacked to the wall in front of my bed and placed them in a small paper shopping bag. My favorite piece of artwork, Eugene's framed eighteen-by-twenty-four-inch pencil-on-paper drawing of photographer Bert Stern's feather picture was carefully packed in bubble wrap and set aside. The large potted pink tulips that Joyce had purchased from the hospital gift shop—silk because live plants were prohibited in the isolation rooms—were placed on top of the cart. The bottom levels were filled with a number of plastic hospital bags marked "This bag belongs to _____," and they had my name filled in with a black Sharpie. Everything I had wanted or needed in these past months was placed on the cart and would soon be incorporated into my real life, which was waiting for me outside. It was humbling to see my existence reduced to such a small collection of inconsequential possessions.

I was soon distracted from this reverie and my family's bustle by the sound of laughter coming from the nurses' station. There I saw a young man, probably in his late teens, who sat and chatted with the nurses. *Another patient,* I thought. I later learned that his name was Steven and he was also battling leukemia.

He was, in fact, the very first patient I had ever seen in the hospital. Like me, he had no hair. However, I slowly realized the differences between us. He had an exuberance about him, as evidenced by his deep belly laughs, which made me uneasy. Although I had also experienced laughter during my stay, much of it courtesy of Sandy and Suzanne, I suppose it was odd to observe it for the first time, especially amidst the cold and sterile backdrop of a hospital setting. It seemed somehow inappropriate to feel such joy in this place.

The patient then stood and began helping the nurses with the food trays, transferring them from a hallway table onto a cart. Tall and thin, he was all legs and arms. He walked briskly from place to place, promptly placing the trays on a cart. He walked about with such quick, fluid movements and held a tray in each of his hands. It was at this moment that I realized the essential difference between us: unlike me, this patient could use both sides of his body.

Although I had been told from the very start that suffering a stroke was unusual for leukemia patients, this information had never sunk in. I didn't want to be so different, so "other," and part of me believed that all leukemia patients also had to deal with issues of physical disability, just like me.

I may have known on some level that confronting this truth would only bring up a whole other set of issues, such as my personal responsibility in all of this. The stroke, after all, could have been avoided if I had trusted what my body was telling me and insisted on getting a second opinion regarding my most severe symptom, the ongoing 104-degree temperature. It was much easier for me to convince myself that all patients' experiences were like mine, dealing with physical disability in addition to cancer. But as this young man stood before me, I could no longer deny that my condition was, in fact, unique.

For one brief instant, I was enraged. I was angry with myself. I was angry with the doctor who had misdiagnosed me. I was angry with God. But most of all, I was angry with this young man who stood before me, seemingly mocking my ill fate. I sat there stunned, all the while intensely staring at the left side of his body, from his arm down to his leg and up again. *Why me? Why is he so lucky?* I thought it over and over. *Why is he so lucky?*

My attention was soon diverted to my family exiting the

During my respite home from the hospital in June 1988, several weeks before my scheduled bone marrow transplant. Seated, from right, Jasmine with Yasi on her lap and me. Eugene is behind me, followed by Genny and Che-Che. Che-Che is looking at me with what appears to be a powerful mixture of love and concern.

room, pushing the cart with my belongings and carrying stray items. "We'd better get going," someone said. "Jasmine and the baby are waiting for us at the lobby, so we better head down." As we made our way around the corner to the elevator, I took a last glance at the plaque that was on the wall next to my room, the one that read "4200," and I never looked back.

"Come on, Armand," I exclaimed to Jasmine's two-year-old son as we exited the lobby's automatic glass doors side by side, I in a wheelchair and he in a stroller. Gleefully, I reached for his hand. "Let's race and see who can get to the car first!" Armand giggled wildly and kicked his feet up and down as we were wheeled into the parking lot. It was a great day. I was going home.

CHAPTER SIXTEEN

A Passageway

My month back home was just as I'd expected, and I savored each day surrounded by the loving support of my family. My married sisters took turns coming by and assisting my mother and the rest of the family with my care, such as helping with my showers or driving me to my outpatient physical therapy appointments. At night, Eugene would sit at my bedside and read to me until I fell fast asleep. *The Velveteen Rabbit* by Margery Williams became one of my favorites. To lighten the tone further, Eugene would read the book's opening line imitating Meryl Streep's voice, just as she narrates on the album she and pianist George Winston released in 1985. "There once was a Velveteen rabbit..."

From the very start, I accepted that my time at home was only temporary. I knew I would be readmitted to the hospital, which helped tremendously when my respite came to an end. I even looked forward to returning, mainly because I'd be reunited with the nurses who had become my friends. Before I knew it, July 15th arrived and I was back in the hospital for the transplant that had the power to cure my leukemia.

"Sorry to interrupt, everyone," Suzanne said as she finished prepping my room one morning shortly before the transplant, "but it's time to get you up and showered, Julie." She held in the crook of one arm a pile of fresh blue-and-white checkered hospital gowns and a supply of white towels, which she promptly placed in the bathroom. Suzanne then removed the roll-away table that still held my empty breakfast tray and wheeled the shower chair into its place, locking the chair by my bedside.

My parents, siblings, and Ali were well aware of the morning drill and quietly gathered their belongings to ensure they didn't get in the way. While my mother always preferred to sit in the waiting room down the hall during my showers so that she was nearby, the others liked to go downstairs to the cafeteria to grab a quick bite to eat.

"I'll have a cup of hot chocolate for you when you're done, honey bun," Daddy assured me as he headed out the door with the others. As part of our morning ritual, Daddy often came to my room with his coffee in one hand and my hot chocolate in the other.

In the month since completing my induction chemotherapy treatment, I always felt cold. Consequently, the thermostat in my room was kept at what is, for many, an unbearable 75 degrees. And still, I always shivered underneath the pile of heated blankets the nurses brought in from time to time. That morning was no exception. Feeling colder than usual, I looked forward to the hot chocolate and dreaded the moment when I'd have to endure the bathroom's cool air before the shower warmed up. When I asked Suzanne to leave the hot shower running for a few minutes before she took me in, she looked at me as though I had momentarily lost my mind.

"In case you haven't heard, *madame*, there is a drought," she bantered. The drought of the late 1980s was one of the worst in Northern California's history.

"Oh, yeah, that, but I'm cold," I whined.

In her usual militant-yet-tender voice, Suzanne replied, "Oh, you'll be fine. You'll see. You won't even think about it in a few minutes."

"Whatever you say, Sarge," I countered.

She then assisted me onto the chair and wheeled me into the bathroom, which was just a few steps from my bed. Besides transporting me from one room to the other, the chair also allowed the nurses to wheel me directly into the large, barrier-free, zero-threshold shower stall, positioning me right underneath the shower head.

I focused on the water's soothing warmth. One minute, Suzanne stood in the shower stall beside me, washing me with a hand towel. The next, she was abruptly wheeling me back to the side of the bed. I later learned that my blood pressure had fallen dramatically and I had lost consciousness.

I was confused when I suddenly found myself out of the shower and on my way back to bed. Had I fallen asleep? How had I gone from the enjoyable, warm shower to being hastily transported? I had no idea, but I didn't wonder for long. My confusion was soon tempered by a remarkable sense of peacefulness and well-being, and I became completely transfixed by Suzanne's every move in the hope of understanding what was happening.

Suzanne locked the shower chair in place. "Julie," she said. "I'm going to get you back in bed." She repeated herself over and over. As she stood on the other side of the bed, facing me, she looked me in the eye and proceeded to straighten and tuck the sheets.

It seemed as if Suzanne's eyes never left me as she hurried about, not even for a moment. She kept saying "I'm going to get you back into bed" as though her voice was a way to keep me alert and keep my attention on her. I soon slumped to the left, my affected side, and realized I was drooling heavily from the left corner of my mouth. I knew something was wrong since I hadn't experienced symptoms like these in months, not since the first critical days after my stroke. The slumping and drooling accelerated Suzanne's movements as she hurriedly folded the blanket down at the top of my bed.

"Julie, I'll have you back in bed in no time," she said once again.

When I was in bed and under the covers, she grabbed the telephone and paged Dr. Wolf to the oncology ward. "Room 4200," she stated. In my tranquil state, I remained focused on Suzanne, calmly watching her. I wondered why she was panicking when, in my mind, there wasn't anything wrong. I was so weak that it didn't occur to me to ask her what was happening. I didn't have the strength to utter a single word.

Once Suzanne hung up, she stood over me and said, "Julie. You need to take a deep breath." This became her mantra for the next several minutes. "I need you to take a deep breath, Julie."

I was so weak that I hadn't noticed my breathing becoming short and shallow. Only when Suzanne pointed it out did I realize that I couldn't take a normal breath. Then, all at once, there was a commotion as Dr. Wolf and other medical staff members entered the room and joined Suzanne at my bedside. My view of the medical team encircling my bed was concave, as if I was looking through a fisheye lens. The space above their heads curved inward, and I couldn't see anything in the periphery.

I was perfectly calm even though something was clearly wrong, which only added to my confusion. Soon, the voices began to sound as if they were calling out from a great distance. Even more strangely, it felt as though I were "behind myself" as I watched the medical team work.

It was an odd sensation, unlike anything I'd ever experienced. I felt as though I were looking out from behind my conscious self—not from directly behind my eyes but from a place deep within, a dark space that seemed cavernous. As I looked at Suzanne and Dr. Wolf from what felt like an enormous distance, there was vast darkness all around me. I don't know if I was simply in a formless place or if I was inside a structure of some kind, but I sensed that wherever it was, it was a passageway. It seemed as if I was at the entrance to a corridor that led to a place much deeper inside of me. I wasn't too far within yet, since I could still see and hear everyone, albeit from a distance, but I sensed that it was possible to slip much further away.

Suzanne's distant voice infiltrated the darkness, drifting through the passageway and bringing me back to the present. She had left my bedside to chastise my mother, who had entered the room. "Mrs. Lee," she said, "I'm going to have to ask you to leave."

Ali and my family had gathered outside of my hospital room during the confusion. The medical team had instructed them to remain behind the circular window that looked in on my room. My mother, not content to watch from afar, had burst in to find out what was happening.

"I am not going anywhere," my mother defiantly declared. "If my daughter is going to *die*, I'm going to be *right* here."

Her tone was the very same one she'd used with us when we were kids—a tone that told us there wasn't any room for compromise. She spoke with such force and conviction that my internal response was, *Perhaps now would be a good time to warn Suzanne that her efforts to keep my mother out will be in vain.*

I couldn't see my mother because the staff was clustered so tightly around my bed, but I heard her at the side of the room, near the door. I imagined her making the demand with her arm authoritatively bent at the elbow, the short strap of her purse hanging from her forearm, her index finger pointing downward as if to underscore her resolve. Even though it was physically impossible for me to see her through the circle of medical professionals, I visualized my mother standing there. The image wasn't clear—it was fuzzy and grainy, as if I was watching the scene on an old television set, and I saw no one else in the room but her. Stranger still, it seemed as if I were looking down at her from somewhere above the room as she pointed and defied official orders. My mother was not going anywhere.

Although I was incredibly weak, my mother's words—"If my daughter is going to *die*"—struck me to the core. Death became an even more abstract idea than it had ever been. I didn't register that this moment could be one of the last moments of my life. "Die" was just a word to me, unattached to any thoughts or emotions.

Yes, I thought. *That's exactly what's happening. I'm dying.*

It was a relief to hear my mother say what had perhaps been on everyone's mind, including—on some level—my own. Her words put an end to my confusion about what was happening. They confirmed a deep knowledge that had been buried inside of me. Yes, I was dying. My mother's courage to speak that truth, rather than keeping silent about it, had brought me closer to the room. I was suddenly back in my bed instead of heading down the passageway, although I was still "behind myself" and far removed from the unfolding drama. As I looked up at the medical team, I once again had a fisheye view of the people looking down at me.

Sensing my mother's fierce determination, or maybe picking up on the message I'd telepathically sent her, Suzanne backed off and rejoined the medical team at my bedside.

"Julie, take a deep breath," Dr. Wolf instructed over and over.

I tried, but I was still so weak that I could only take small breaths. Dr. Wolf wasn't having it. He finally raised his voice in frustration and sternly said, "JULIE. TAKE A DEEP BREATH."

My response was immediate. I don't know what changed so that I could breathe again, but I inhaled deeply and soon felt like myself—as though I were looking out at the world from directly behind my eyes. Regaining my normal perspective is the last thing I can recall from that morning.

In the days and weeks that followed, I talked about the experience with anyone who would listen. I especially enjoyed hearing my mother's version of the events since her story corroborated my own. We processed it together by retelling our stories.

"They told us to wait outside," my mother explained, "but I didn't care what they said. Even though Ali, Daddy, and the others tried to stop me, I told them *NO* and went straight into your room anyway and told that nurse—the one with the braids—*I am not going anywhere…*"

I wasn't prepared to deal with the emotional impact of the experience, so I focused on the details of the event as it had unfolded. I knew on a gut level that it was a moment I needed to remember. I have heard of near-death experiences, yet I cannot say if that is what I went through. Although the skeptics and medical professionals have theories to explain such an occurrence (for instance, lack of oxygen to the brain), I've often wondered if the sense of being "behind myself" could have been the initial stage before "the tunnel" and "the light," experiences that many others have had. I suppose I will never know. All I know for certain is that the sublime sensations of peacefulness, security, and warmth were palpable. Because of that, death doesn't frighten me. I know that I will be in a state of total acceptance and peace when I die, so nothing else will matter.

I am also certain that if I had died, the mere sound of my mother's voice would have sustained and guided me through whatever stages were ahead. The strength and power in her words would have been a beacon. Simply put, I wasn't afraid because my mother was with me. I knew I'd be fine because she would, as always, ensure my safe passage.

CHAPTER SEVENTEEN

A Long, Dark Night

On the morning of my scheduled transplant, Sandy prepared me for what was the final leg of my treatment plan: the high-dose chemotherapy. I had completed the radiation therapy about a week earlier without incident. When the chemotherapy was completed, I would essentially be without a functioning immune system for a little while, allowing Che-Che's marrow to be infused a few days later, once I'd recovered from the side effects. It would be a non-surgical procedure. If things went as planned, I would finally be released from the hospital and go home for good.

"I'm going to give you something that will help put you to sleep and I'll also insert a urinary catheter, so hopefully you'll be asleep for the next few hours throughout the chemo treatment," Sandy explained.

"Really? A catheter?" I was incredulous. A catheter made perfect sense, but I was taken aback that I hadn't thought about how such basic matters would be addressed during the arduous procedure. Up to that point, the medical team's primary focus had been ensuring that my family and I fully understood the risks and complications of the transplant itself. We hadn't discussed minor details.

The best way to summarize the wealth of information we received is the bank of keywords I had repeatedly heard since my diagnosis: high-risk treatment, high-dose chemotherapy, high-dose total body irradiation, life-threatening complications such as infections, and the dreaded graft-versus-host disease (GVHD), which occurs when the donated marrow perceives that it is not in its own environment and therefore attacks the host patient's tissues. From the very start, I listened and took in the information. I wasn't alarmed by the grim prospects because the stroke's side effects continued to be my main concern. Besides, I viewed the transplant as getting me one step closer to my ultimate goal of returning home. The way I saw it, the transplant was truly the final hurdle for me.

Sandy continued preparing for the treatment as I slowly drifted to sleep. I thought, *After today, I'll be one step closer to returning home.*

Hours later, I jolted awake. My eyes were wide open before I even realized I was up, as though I knew something big was about to occur. Disoriented, I didn't even know where I was. Then, in a split-second, a wave of nausea unlike any other jarred my memory into place. *Yes,* I thought, *it's the day of my transplant and the high-dose chemotherapy.*

Dull light from the sun's glare filtered through the pink curtains that were drawn in my room; it was probably around noon or so, I surmised. Severe nausea quickly overwhelmed me. Because I was unable to physically sit up on my own, I lifted my head off the pillow as far as I could towards my chest and instinctively cupped my hand over my mouth, as if doing so would somehow stop the inevitable. I began to vomit violently.

"Hey, Julie, I'm right here—I've got you," Sandy softly said as she held my shoulders and brought me to a sitting position. As I sat up, I noticed splotches of a dark stain on my bedsheets and on the top half of my dampened hospital gown. When I brought my hand closer to my face, I saw that it was also covered with the same dark stain: blood. Dazed, I couldn't ask Sandy to explain what was happening to me, so I used my eyes to communicate. I looked at my hand, then looked up at Sandy with wide eyes and furrowed brows, pleading as best I could. Why am I vomiting blood? What's happening to me?

With my palm still face up and coated with the dark stain, Sandy grabbed hold of my hand and wiped it down with a warm washcloth. She said, tenderly but firmly, "It's all right, Julie. You just lie back down, and I'll get you cleaned up." *She doesn't seem concerned,* I thought, *so I guess I'm fine.* I then closed my eyes and instantly fell back into a deep sleep.

When I suddenly awoke to vomit once again—one of many fleeting moments of consciousness brought on by my severe nausea—Sandy explained that she needed to drain the fluid in my lungs. Because I'd been vomiting while sleeping on my back, fluid had collected. Sandy held a long, thin tube and explained, "I'm going to put this tube through your nose, Julie. It'll be quick and painless. Ready?"

Oh no, I thought. *That's the procedure Ali once had, which he described as agonizing.* Filled with dread, I braced myself as best I could. As I sat hunched over in bed, I shut my eyes, took a breath in, and grabbed hold of the railing on the side of the bed. Interestingly, I have no recollection of what it was like to have a tube shoved up my nose and down my throat, which speaks to my very poor condition that day. It must have been quick and painless, just as Sandy had described.

The next time I regained consciousness, night had fallen. It was the first time I woke up without having to vomit, so I knew my treatment was progressing. *It's almost over,* I thought in relief. A nurse—I do not recall which one—was in the room checking the beeping monitors beside my bed. It was dark except for the light coming through the window of the cubicle door. On the other side of the glass, my mother stood in front of other family members who had gathered. She placed her hand against the window and smiled softly, her mouth closed, to get my attention; she then placed the tips of her fingers over her mouth as though to contain her emotion. Soon after, everything again went dark.

About twenty-four hours after the high-dose chemo treatment—on the day of the actual transplant when Che-Che's marrow was to be infused via my catheter—I was in bed watching television. Ali and a couple of family members were in the room with me. Sandy held an infusion bag that was filled with a dark red substance.

"Here it is," Sandy said, "this is your sister's marrow." I thought of Che-Che and what she must have gone through. I knew she was in the hospital somewhere, recovering from the surgical procedure performed earlier that morning to collect her marrow. The procedure was the same one that had been used for the biopsies I had undergone numerous times; however, since a large amount of marrow was obtained, Che-Che had been placed under general anesthesia. She would experience minor soreness on her hipbone, but it was considered a noninvasive procedure and she would be released later that day.

"I'll connect the bag to your catheter now," Sandy explained.

I was astounded by the actual transplant procedure itself. After the donor marrow's cells are infused into the patient's blood, the cells eventually—in about two to four weeks—find their way to the marrow cavities in the patient's bones. The cells then grow and produce new white blood cells, red blood cells, and platelets.

Early the next morning, I found Suzanne at the foot of my bed, writing something on the whiteboard that hung on the

wall directly in front of me. I had just woken up, so I was
surprised that I was alert and felt rather good—almost normal,
the way I'd felt before the transplant.

I was curious to see what Suzanne had written. "Good
morning," she began when she headed towards my bedside.
"You're doing great, Julie." I then caught a glimpse of what she
had written: "WBC 0."

"That there," Suzanne explained as she pointed to the
whiteboard, "is your white blood count as of today, which is
zero." I was surprised by this number since the average normal
range is between 3,500 and 10,500 white blood cells per
microliter of blood. "Once that count goes up and you begin
eating again, *you* can go home."

Home, I thought. I would do anything to be home again.

"And remember to visualize your white blood cells increas-
ing," Suzanne advised.

Today, bone marrow transplant patients with a white blood
count of zero are prescribed medications that can help the body
produce cells. In 1988, however, the immune boosters were not
yet available. Visualization was certainly not part of the post-
treatment protocol, but it was recommended in passing by
some of the nurses. Using mental imagery made sense to me,
and I started the practice on day one after my transplant.

As I lay in bed, I closed my eyes and pictured my white
blood cells as round figures with stick arms, hands, and legs
walking about inside their home—my bones. I imagined them
as they prepared to welcome Che-Che's marrow. *Her marrow has
to feel at home so it can begin producing healthy blood cells,* I thought.
Therefore, each one of my stick figures had an assigned task.
There was one, for instance, who opened the front door of my
bones and placed a brown coir "Welcome" mat outside.
Another fluffed up the intricately-patterned plush pillows on

the overstuffed couch and armchairs. Yet another was tasked with turning on the lamps to cast a soft light in the living room. Lastly, another stick figure steadily stoked the fire in the hearth.

Visualization came naturally to me and I enjoyed it immensely. Like my stick figures, who were each assigned a task, I saw my daily practice of eating, sleeping, and visualizing as the only tasks that I had to complete as I rested and recovered. Three times a day, after each meal, over and over, that scene went through my mind.

The scene I pictured was similar to an animation that one might find on YouTube today to help patients and their families understand a bone marrow transplant, but mine occurred in the time before the Information Age. I still have the booklet that the hospital provided to Ali and my family in order to help them understand the procedure. Entitled *Research Report: Bone Marrow Transplantation*, it was an invaluable resource for everyone. Now, decades later, the booklet looks as though it had been passed from one person to the next for careful review. Even Yasi had gotten it at some point. Underneath the title heading on the front cover is a pencil drawing of a large, misshapen smiley face with a set of misshapen round eyes.

And, of course, the booklet was a resource for Ali, who often had it with him. It was in his hands when he asked Dr. Wolf one morning, "It's my understanding that after the transplant, doctor, it will take about two to four weeks before the marrow settles in and begins producing new blood cells. As you know, we had planned to be married in September." When he spoke, Ali fumbled with the booklet and eventually folded it lengthwise in half. "With the transplant scheduled in July, doctor, do you think it's still possible to keep that date?"

"It's hard to say," Dr. Wolf began, "but it would be cutting it close. We really must wait and see how it goes. For now, I'd recommend postponing the wedding."

"I see," Ali said as he tightened his grip on the folded booklet, then looked at me with a tender half-smile.

Today the booklet's frayed edges, along with the retro font that looks as though it was typed on a typewriter, are reminders of how many years have passed. What's more, the booklet's margins are littered with notes and arrows, and certain words or sentences are either highlighted or underlined with a pencil, silent cues that show me now the matters that jumped out at Ali and my family back then.

One paragraph stands apart from all the rest since it's completely highlighted with a yellow marker. As if to further emphasize its importance, the paragraph is also cordoned off from the rest of the text with hand-drawn brackets on either side. There is even a sizable question mark penciled in the margin. It reads:

> Interstitial pneumonia is another major cause of illness and death. About half the pneumonias are caused by cytomegalovirus infections, which have been fatal in about 80 percent of the cases. This is the most common cause of death in transplant patients.

Only one sentence is highlighted in the booklet's conclusion, as though the reader wanted to ensure it stood out:

> Bone marrow transplantation has been shown to improve long-term survival for patients with diseases such as acute leukemia.

PART THREE

WISER AND STRONGER
THAN YOU WERE BEFORE

CHAPTER EIGHTEEN

Submerged

My eyes were drawn to the multitude of candles that lined the cathedral wall. The one I'd lit sat in the center of the top row amidst a sea of flickering flames. I wondered how my prayer could be heard when it was only one small request among what was perhaps a million cries for mercy the world over. And yet I was comforted in knowing that I was not alone in my despair, comforted in knowing that we all have moments when we feel like the Forgotten Ones. These moments, I'd later learn, would pass, just like everything else in life. The question is, how does one hang on until they do?

The ritual of mass had little significance in my life when I was growing up, but as I became older—especially after the transplant—I found great comfort simply sitting in church and praying. With all that is going on in the world, a church is perhaps the only space that's quiet enough to allow the heavens to hear us. Equally comforting was the ritual of lighting a candle. It was my assurance, I suppose, that I had His complete attention—at least for that moment.

Although Ali is a Muslim, he nevertheless made use of the time we spent in the cathedral that day, shortly after my release from the hospital. With his head lowered, he held my hand tightly. We sat in silence asking—no, imploring—God for mercy. Since returning home, I had focused more on the here and now, on the practical matters such as adjusting to life with my physical limitations. Surely, even God must know of the anguish I felt because of my now-broken body.

Please, dear Lord, I prayed. *Please just let all of this be a bad dream. I beg you; let me wake up to find that this isn't really happening, please.* I pleaded so intensely that my eyes began to well up. Although I wasn't verbalizing my thoughts, it seemed for one small moment as though my voice were echoing throughout the empty church.

I wanted a quick fix for my sorrow, for it was simply too painful to feel my emotions. Would things ever be the way they were before I got sick? Would I ever be who I used to be? I went to bed with my "new body" each night and awoke with it each morning—a body I did not belong in. A terrible mistake had occurred. I had been placed in this heavy and veritably useless shell. There were no moments when I could forget what had happened because my left side was my constant reminder. I imagined that if I'd just had a leukemia diagnosis, it would be easier to move forward as though it never happened. *God, I don't want this! Help me find a way out. I beg you, give me a miracle.*

And what better place would there be to have one than in His house? That's probably why I spent so much time in churches early in my recovery. I thought perhaps there was some truth in what I'd always believed as a child, that churches were a place of wondrous events. Yet I sensed there wouldn't be a miracle in store for me—not the way I would have wanted, anyway. For some reason, I was stuck on this idea and I had no other choice than to deal with my agony. Why?

I'd been unaware of deep suffering before my stroke and diagnosis. Although I had surely heard of it, I didn't ever imagine that I'd experience it—and certainly not to such an extent. The closest I'd ever come to suffering had been looking at it from afar, the way I viewed my mother's anguish when Papa died, and then turning away when it became too unbearable. Once I grew ill, I no longer had that luxury. I was overwhelmed, and as I slowly discovered, there wasn't anything I could do about it.

The illness had taken away yet another illusion in my life. However, unlike any of my previous losses—for instance, when my family's money disappeared—I wasn't able to pretend that nothing had happened. My physical body was a constant external reminder. This, above all, made it difficult for me to see survival as a blessing. It was no wonder that depression slowly took hold.

It became especially obvious on occasions that should have felt joyous, like Yasi's fifth birthday. "Happy birthday, dear Yasi, happy birthday to you," we all sang. My family stood encircling the dining table while I was comfortably seated beside my niece. She looked up and exclaimed, "For me?!" Then she blew out the candles on her cake.

Ali stood behind me with his hands on my shoulders as I leaned against him. His loving touch always reassured me that he was there for me. It made me feel centered and balanced despite all that I was going through. It was a picture-perfect moment: Everyone around me was smiling and happy. Anyone looking at me as I sang along would have thought that I was happy too, but I felt empty inside. I thought, *how can I feel so lonely when I'm in a room filled with those I love the most in the world and who love me?* I was lonely even when I wasn't physically alone, something I had never previously experienced. Looking back now, I believe it was due to the disconnect I felt after my illness—no one understood the loss I had endured, myself included. I was also still trying to make sense of all that had happened.

Even my dreams came to reflect my ever-increasing sorrow. At the time, mine were so powerful that dreaming became something new for me. In the past, I hadn't remembered most of my dreams—and when I did, they held little meaning. After the transplant, my dreams became vivid and illuminating.

One dream, in particular, made me understand the depths of my despair. In it, I sensed that death was all around me. Seated in the backseat of a black limousine, I noticed that everything seemed to be enormous while I appeared to be a miniaturized version of my adult self. My feet didn't even touch the car's floor. Visible through the front window was a long, winding road ahead, leading towards a hilltop. The clouds were dark and foreboding and it was about to storm.

A cascade of white flowers hung on the rearview mirror, and they contrasted sharply with the shadowy figure—a silhouette of a man—who was seated up front. He was dressed in a black suit and chauffeur's cap, and his skin was dark gray with deep pockmarks. Although he frightened me, I screamed at him at the top of my lungs. Over and over, I cried, "Damn it! Drive faster! You're going too slowly! Do you hear me? Drive FASTER!" Despite my rage, my voice was weak and the driver did not respond. He continued to gaze straight ahead, smirking as he drove at the same slow speed. It appeared that death would not come at my behest.

As we continued up the hill, I looked out my window and saw a woman standing by the roadside, her eyes downcast. I was immediately struck by the long, blonde hair that fell to her waist. Even though it was cloudy, a bright light illuminated her golden hair. My eyes were then drawn to the splotches of color on her black top, including a piercing blue and a vibrant yellow. The colors were so full of life that they, along with the light and her hair, overpowered everything else about her, including the details of her face.

Suddenly, my dream began to move in slow motion. It was as if I could see every individual frame in a film as she lifted her head to look up at me, wisps of her hair blowing in the breeze. Our eyes met and she smiled softly as the car moved slowly past her, frame by frame. Her smile left me with a profound sense of hope. She seemed to know something that I did not.

The woman would resurface years later, after I'd come through my depression, although I didn't recognize her at first. It happened when I first began writing about my illness and recovery, an idea about which I had considerable doubt. I was so uncertain that I hadn't mentioned the idea to anyone other than Eugene. I thought, *Who am I to write my story?*

"Hey Euge," I said one morning as we sat down for breakfast. "I have to tell you about the weird dream I had last night."

He leaned in, listening intently.

"I was showing a woman out the door of the house when she suddenly turned, looked me in the eye, pointed her finger right at my face, and said, 'Oh, and *don't* forget to write that *book*!'" I pointed at Eugene's face just as the woman had done to me in the dream. She had said it with such conviction that it stunned me. Even in the hazy logic that accompanies dreams, I wondered how she knew about my book.

"Wait a minute," Eugene said as he took a sip of coffee. "Who is this woman?"

"That's just it. I have no idea who she is!"

"Well, describe her to me," Eugene said.

"I don't know...she was tall and thin with long, blonde hair." I paused as the revelation hit me. "Oh my God," I exclaimed. "She was that same woman in my other dream, the one when I was riding in the car! She had that same long, blonde, wavy hair down to her waist!"

Who was she and how did she know of my longing to tell my story? I sensed that she was a guide of some kind, someone who had been there from the very start of my whole ordeal to help me get through each day and who continued to make herself known to me when I needed her most.

CHAPTER NINETEEN

Resurfacing

It has been said that we essentially have no control over our emotions. In other words, when we're feeling down, there really isn't a whole lot we can do about it. The one thing we *do* have control over is our actions. So, for example, rather than sitting at home when we're feeling sad, we can choose to do an activity of some kind. This concept came naturally to me. Fortunately, I was still able to make choices that helped me to get through my recovery.

Fueled from the very start by what I can only describe as an energy more fierce than any I'd never known, I primarily focused on activities that would aid in my physical rehabilitation. Everything I did took my mind off my troubles, and I found it to be empowering. The next several months required nothing less than discipline, resolve, and plain hard work. Physical activity provided the structure I needed in order to move forward.

I was standing at the shallow end of a rectangular lap pool trying not to glance at the other people in my swimming class when one of my classmates introduced herself. "I was 79 years old when I had my stroke and I'd always wanted to learn how to swim," Lorraine said. "So when my physical therapist told me about this class, I signed up immediately." It was my first time attending the class, which was designed for people with disabilities, and Lorraine and I chatted during a break from the kicking drills that a volunteer instructor had assigned to us.

"I must say that it's hard to believe *you* had a stroke—why, you're just a baby. You're much too young!" Lorraine tightened the chin strap of her beige latex swimming cap.

"Yes, I am." I nodded in agreement. Indeed, I was the youngest one in a class filled with men and women who all appeared to be over sixty. Steam rose from the heated pool and the smell of chlorine hung heavily in the room. I looked around me and felt a sharp pang of despair. Although I was different from my classmates because I was much younger than they were, we also had one undeniable commonality. We walked and held our bodies in the same manner. As they walked into the pool area from the changing rooms, their affected legs swung out to the side, just like mine, and their curled arms and clenched hands pressed tightly against their chests, just like mine. I didn't see myself as one of them, and yet I was. For most of the first class, I focused on the instructor and avoided looking at the others as much as possible.

Despite my discomfort, I attended the two classes offered each week, and within a short time, I was doing twenty laps freestyle. It was an amazing feat since I hadn't been able to master freestyle when I first learned to swim as a teenager. I could never complete a full freestyle lap back then, so I always reverted to my favorite, the breaststroke, halfway through. However, my illness left me physically unable to do the breaststroke and forced me to learn the style that had once evaded me. Incredibly, over a decade later and with literally only half the strength I once had, I was effortlessly completing the laps.

To my dismay, however, swimming did not directly benefit the rehabilitation of my affected side. In other words, being so active no longer led to any noticeable rewards. Yet I continued to attend the classes because swimming was the one activity I could do with relative speed.

Although I swam a lot, my primary activity during this time was a Home Program I'd designed with the help of my physical therapist. It consisted of arm and leg stretches and long walks by the Bay. Looking back on it today, its benefit was twofold: there were physical rewards, but the program was equally beneficial to my emotional wellbeing (if not more so). My days were structured. Typically up by 6:00 a.m., I reserved the morning hours solely for my program and scheduled all medical appointments for later in the day. Since I was well enough at that point to take care of myself while those around me went to work, I had my own agenda, which gave me a sense of purpose.

With Ali away during the week, it was my father who served as the primary coach for my Home Program. As we strolled the boardwalk that ran alongside our condominium, he always walked patiently beside me, prepared to assist in case I lost my balance. I vaguely recalled what it was like to move without having to remind myself to remain relaxed. How could it be that after years of functioning without such concerns, I was unable to remember what it felt like?

Even when I tried focusing on the way the right side of my body moved and felt in hopes of reminding my affected side of how easy it all really was, it became clear that the left side was no longer "connected" to me—an idea that I had been slowly coming to accept in the months that had passed since the stroke. As such, my movements were calculated. I had never known that so many different parts of the body are used to take one simple step. I had to tell myself, for instance, to keep my hip down and both shoulders parallel, which somehow made it easier to bring my foot forward when taking a step. Besides relying less on a cane, another gauge for my progress was when I began requiring less assistance from others.

When I was at last able to go out for walks by myself, they were invaluable on days when I felt down or sorry for myself. Looking back on it today, those walks reaffirmed the notion that while it may seem like we do not have a choice during trying times, we *do* ultimately have a choice. On such occasions, I'd tell myself, even if I had to say it out loud, "Okay, you're feeling sad, but feel that way while you're out walking." I soon realized that getting some fresh air and looking out at the Bay helped to change my mood. By the end of the walks, I always felt more at peace—not necessarily happier, but the walking quieted my mind.

These solitary walks provided me with time for deep introspection as I attempted to piece my life together. To my surprise, I began to see my life as a story with a beginning, a middle, and—in many ways—an end. It seemed that each event throughout my lifetime, good and bad, from my childhood up to the illness, led to the next, taking me to the place where I now found myself. And the underlying question in my mind was, for what purpose? I sensed that it is only through "making meaning" that one can comprehend and ultimately accept the unthinkable.

During my daily treks, I was always mindful of my hip placement. If I didn't consciously bring my hip forward, the subsequent swing of my leg seemed more evident. I also reminded myself that my shoulders had to remain parallel. Then I would feel the breeze as it brushed my face and it was as if I was suddenly lighter, without a care in the world. And while elderly citizens passed me again and again, I'd inhale the sea air deep into my lungs and then slowly exhale. *It's all right*, I'd think to myself. *We're all headed the same way. I'm just going to get there a little later than everyone else.*

*With my parents in the early 1990s during the early years of my recovery
as I attempted to piece together my life.*

The walks also brought about another revelation. When I would look too far down a challenging path—an incline or a graveled area, for instance—my mind would anticipate the difficulties before me. *Oh no*, I'd think. *I can't walk on gravel.* My weakened ankle would flop and my entire affected side would tense up even more, making it impossible to take the next step forward. I discovered that I had to simply stop in these moments, look into the Bay, and take a deep breath to calm myself. I'd focus on the seagulls' distant caws, which had been background noise only a moment before, and the tension in my body would instantly lessen. Only then would my left foot relax and fall back to a more neutral position, making it possible to take another step and proceed on my walk. And so I'd push on, inhaling and exhaling all the while.

Mindful breathing was what they called it. Breathing itself had taken on new meaning. I realized I could easily become overwhelmed, so I breathed. It was as though I were releasing my despair with each exhalation.

At some point, I discovered that if I kept my gaze on the perimeter of each step I took, it helped to keep my mind—and therefore my body—in a more relaxed state. I slowly learned that the trick was to never look too far ahead, an idea that was so simple it could be applied to the rest of my life as well. If I looked too far into the future to contemplate the unknowns that lay ahead, I could easily become overwhelmed.

My journey had begun with a reading foretelling all that was to follow. Perhaps the time had now come to begin living in the moment.

CHAPTER TWENTY

Steven

Although I had been released from the hospital about a month after the transplant, I made regular appearances at the cancer center for follow-up visits. "There's a young man I think you should meet—another patient who also had a stroke," Nancy—one of the clinic nurses—said as she examined me during one of my visits.

"Young man?" I asked incredulously. "Wait a minute. What is this young man's name?"

"Steven," Nancy answered matter-of-factly.

I pictured the young patient who had put food trays onto a cart the day I was discharged from the hospital for the first time, the one who was all arms and legs and who walked with such quick, fluid movements.

"You mean…the young man who I saw outside my room also had a stroke?" I sat on the examination table in disbelief, repeatedly asking her to confirm that I'd heard correctly.

"Yes, he's the one. Steven. He's upstairs right now. The nurses are celebrating his birthday."

I was appalled. Steven's disease had returned because he didn't have a bone marrow donor. It came back with such a vengeance that he suffered a stroke.

It was hard to process. I had, after all, deemed him as "the Lucky One." Strokes didn't happen to the lucky ones. I quickly cycled through a range of emotions. Shock. Also, sadness and compassion. A stroke isn't a predicament that I would want to happen to anyone, especially someone as young and full of vitality as Steven. Yet I was also comforted by knowing that my situation wasn't so unusual after all, and it felt good to know I wasn't alone. The revelation was fleeting, however; it seemed inappropriate to feel relieved by Steven's situation.

When my father went to get the car after my appointment, I waited by the lobby entrance. I wore my full leg brace, and I had a firm grip on my four-legged cane to ensure I maintained my balance. Suddenly, the nearby elevator dinged. A crowd exited and quickly disbursed. Among the crowd was an older woman who pushed a wheelchair occupied by a gaunt young man. The dark circles under his eyes made them appear sunken. It was Steven.

As he and the woman rushed past me, Steven looked me in the eye as if to acknowledge my anguish. I sensed that he knew as much about me as I did about him.

I wanted to call out to him and introduce myself, but it was shocking to see what he had become. Our roles had been reversed. I was now standing while he was in a wheelchair. Dumbfounded, all I could do was to stare with my mouth hanging open. To my dismay, Steven and the woman pushing his wheelchair quickly exited the automatic lobby doors.

A moment later, the woman returned to the lobby. She was alone, and she headed straight toward me. As she approached, I realized she wasn't as old as she had appeared from afar, but fatigue was written across her face. She looked as though she hadn't had much sleep in quite a while. Her gray, shoulder-length hair also added to the effect, but up close I could see the smoothness of her skin and just a few lines on her face.

"Hi," she said. "Are you Julie?"

"Yes," I replied.

"Hi. I'm Steven's mother. I wanted to meet you to let you know that you've been a household name in our home for the last few weeks now. How long did it take you to recover after your stroke, to begin walking again? When did you first regain movement?" My instincts had been correct. Steven's family *had* heard my story.

She looked at me, and then her eyes subtly trailed down my leg, as though she were in awe that I was standing on my own.

"It took about a month," I said, "before I was able to lift my leg up off the bed."

"Really?" Her eyes lit up with hope.

I was so overwhelmed with emotion that I don't remember now most of what was said between us, or even how our brief encounter ended.

After I learned of Steven's stroke, he often entered my thoughts. One day, when I'd once again been passed by the elderly during my walk, I imagined how Steven would have responded. I pictured him wearing a baseball cap like me but using a quad cane as he re-discovered his body, since he wasn't as far along as I was in terms of recovering from his stroke. I imagined bantering with him about being passed by senior citizens. Because of the light-hearted personality I'd observed the first time I saw him, I pictured him telling a joke: "Slower than an octogenarian with ankle weights!" I was sure we would have shared a sense of humor and laughed at ourselves rather than wallowing in self-pity.

A month after meeting Steven's mother, I saw him again— this time, in a dream. I knew I was dreaming as the scene unfolded before me. I had heard of lucid dreams, but this was my first time experiencing one.

In the dream, I stood before a circular window that looked in on a hospital isolation room that I sensed was not my own.

The room was white from floor to ceiling, intensely lit from overhead. The bed was surrounded by members of a medical team who were dressed in white from head to toe. They wore white headgear and white jumpsuits. They even wore white booties and gloves.

I homed in on the patient laying on the bed—a bald, pale, and emaciated young man with dark circles outlining his sunken eyes. It was Steven.

The white bedsheet was pulled up to his chin and his head was propped on pillows. Steven looked at me and our eyes instantly locked. He didn't blink, and his penetrating stare seemed to make his head tremble.

Even though I remained on the other side of the glass window, peering in, his searing gaze made me feel as though I were suddenly closer to him. As I looked into his eyes, I knew what he was thinking and feeling, as though we were one. Steven was dying and he wanted me to pay close attention, to fully understand his thoughts and feelings as he slipped away.

Steven wasn't afraid, just as I wasn't afraid during my own brush with death. But unlike me, Steven had a fierce desire to live. I could sense him desperately holding on to his life. He did not want to die.

I had the dream during the early months of my recovery at home, when I first wondered whether death would have been preferable to surviving. The question arose from dealing with the profound issues of loss and grief that came along with my survival, accompanied by the practical concerns of living with a physical disability.

Months later, during a follow-up visit at the cancer center, I asked Nancy about Steven. "Unfortunately," she began, "Steven didn't have a match. He didn't have a donor, so we couldn't proceed with the transplant. He died a couple of months ago. It's hit some of us nurses really hard." Her eyes were downcast.

"Oh no," I said. "That's terrible news. I wanted so much to meet him, but I never got the chance."

"Yeah, I know. You've always asked about him," Nancy said.

I was blindsided by the news. I sat on the examination table in stunned silence as Nancy proceeded with the exam. I was shocked by another dramatic parallel between my journey and Steven's: my dream. I'd had it two months earlier, around the time Steven died.

I felt guilty. Guilty for coveting, during our first encounter, the fact that Steven "just" had leukemia to deal with but no physical deficits from a stroke. And guilt for the rage I'd felt as I stared at the left side of his body, moving freely as he prepared the food trays, while I asked over and over, *Why me? Why is he so lucky?*

And, admittedly, I was riddled with guilt for the small comfort I felt when I later learned that Steven had also suffered a stroke. It's rare to come across others who have experienced catastrophic loss—let alone two catastrophic, back-to-back diagnoses—as I had been repeatedly reminded in the early months. My medical team didn't know of another leukemia patient who had suffered a stroke, or even a stroke patient under the age of 50, for that matter. The anomalies had made it easy for me to feel as if I had been targeted, and feeling targeted made me feel even more cut off in the inherently isolating world of illness and disability.

After I was released from the hospital, I scoured bookstores and libraries in search of stories that reflected my own, but with little success. The one book I did eventually find was by actress Patricia Neal, who had recently released her memoir *As I Am*.

Neal's book chronicled a series of strokes that began at the age of forty. I couldn't connect with her story, though. She was from my mother's generation and had been much older than I was at the time of her stroke. Unlike me, she had a family of her own—a husband and children.

What's more, no matter how much support I received from my family, my friends, and Ali, my unusual and negative circumstances made me feel as though I stood apart from everyone else. While I had been lying in a hospital bed and learning to walk all over again, my peers were launching new beginnings: marriages, careers, parenthood. A part of me felt left out, like I no longer fit in anywhere. It had been reassuring to know that Steven was out there, dealing with circumstances exactly like mine.

A part of me clung to Steven as though he were a lifeline keeping me afloat. The similarities between our situations were dramatic and uncanny, which made me feel that I did, in fact, still belong somewhere. Connecting with just one other human being on such a powerful level, even though we never met, was enough to help me eventually reconnect with those around me. Knowing Steven's plight made me feel less isolated. I had not been targeted after all. Bad things do sometimes happen, even to the *lucky* ones.

Our lives had intersected at a pivotal moment, as if to offer one another inspiration in our darkest hours. And although we never met, losing Steven felt like losing an old, dear friend. I sometimes thought about what it would have been like if we had known each other. When I took long walks by the Bay during the early part of my recovery, I continued to imagine Steven there, walking alongside me. Only he would have understood the effort and resolve behind taking that one step forward.

As the lone survivor, I felt an obligation to honor Steven's life in some way, and I also wanted to acknowledge the impact he had on mine. In 2016, many years after Steven's death, I attended an annual cancer survivor event that was sponsored by the cancer center I had so often visited for follow-up appointments during my recovery. I walked by the cancer center's "survivor tent" that morning. Suddenly, Gretchen—one of the nurses who had cared for me so many years earlier and who was still on staff at the hospital—emerged from the crowd and approached me.

"Hey, Julie—you look great!" Gretchen exclaimed.

We hugged as I responded. "Oh, Gretchen, thank you! It's always so good to see you!"

"So, how many years has it been now since your treatment?" she asked.

"Unbelievably, I'm 28 years post-transplant!" I proudly replied.

"Wow! That is unbelievable!" Gretchen said.

Then Mary, one of the hospital staff members who had been tasked with coordinating activities for the day, called out to me. "Hey, Juliane, don't forget to sign our survivor banner. Hopefully that will get others to sign it!"

"Yes, of course!" I replied.

To highlight the impact cancer has made on people's lives, the event attendees were encouraged to sign a large banner, either as a survivor or in honor or in memory of someone who battled cancer.

I walked to the display table that held the white, plastic, six-foot banner and selected a bright orange marker from the collection of colorful Sharpies strewn across the table. Shielding my eyes as best I could from the bright morning sun, I chose a blank spot on the bottom corner and wrote in bold print,

"Juliane 1988." As I always did when attending such events, I also wrote, "Steven 1988" alongside my own name.

CHAPTER TWENTY-ONE

The Storytellers

As part of my immersion into recovery, I attended a stroke workshop in San Francisco that featured a panel of survivor speakers. My father drove up to the entrance of the event center.

"Let Daddy walk you in," my mother said.

"No. No, I can do this on my own," I replied. It was the first occasion that I would be out in the world unaccompanied by Ali or my family, and I was excited about the prospect of getting around on my own. I had called for information weeks in advance to plan ahead. I was pleased to see there weren't any steps to the automatic front doors, just as I'd been told.

"We'll be back at two and we'll be right here waiting for you," Daddy said.

When I entered the meeting room, I scanned it quickly for an aisle seat near an exit, for easy access. My decision to arrive early was a good one, since most of the folding chairs were still available. I took a seat and carefully leaned my cane against the chair in front of me as the room slowly filled.

Even in the early stages of my recovery, I sensed that healing involves not only the physical but the emotional as well, and everyone in the room had a story to tell. This not only confirmed my understanding of healing, but it also confirmed the power of stories, which I'd learned when I was a young girl listening to my mother's tales of her own childhood. And I had been again reminded of storytelling's importance when I came across Steven. I once read that it is the telling and retelling of our stories that can help bring us to a place of healing, which is why talk therapy plays a vital role in the grief process. What's more, storytelling can be healing for both the speaker and the listener, thus its extraordinary impact.

As I listened to the presenters, I was comforted and reassured to know that I hadn't been specifically targeted by my stroke or my leukemia, so to speak—awful things could happen to anyone. I was reminded, once again, that sorrow, like happiness, is simply a part of life.

One speaker, Rod McLean[1], spoke of the stroke he'd had over two decades earlier, at age twenty. Mainly affecting his mobility on the right side of his body, the stroke had rendered him aphasic, a condition that occurs when the speech center of the brain is affected. "It's as if all the words I'd known were in a file cabinet and someone has tossed the files out in a room," Rod explained. "The words feel like they're at the tip of my tongue, but I just can't seem to find them." I was astounded. *Aphasia,* I thought. *Now that would be tough.*

Having a stroke is like playing a game of roulette. It can occur in any area of the brain, damaging the part that controls mobility, the part that controls speech, or even, in cases that involve the brain stem, the part that controls breathing itself. Stroke was, as I learned that morning, the third leading cause of death in the United States, with cancer at number two behind

---

[1] *Interested readers may learn more about Rod's experience in* Stroke Survivors, *the book he co-authored with William H. Bergquist and Barbara A. Kobylinski, published by Jossey-Bass, San Francisco, 1994.*

the frontrunner, heart disease. I had survived two of the country's leading causes of death at the time.

Rod ended by saying, "I remember when the doctors told me that I would never be able to use my arm again. Well, look at me." He held his once-affected arm to the side and moved it up and down.

I was silent as clapping and cheers filled the room, momentarily stunned and immensely joyful. At long last, someone affirmed the idea that anything is possible. With a wide grin on my face, I thought, *Yes, there's hope for me yet*. I joined the applauding crowd by slapping my hand against my thigh. I later met Rod, who validated my struggles.

By December of 1988—five months after my transplant—I triumphantly achieved my objective: I no longer used a cane and could get around just wearing an ankle brace. I made this gradual transition by first switching from a quad cane to a cane with a standard tip as a base. Eventually, I began to rely less on the cane by making a deliberate effort not to lean on it as much. At times, I even held it a few inches off the ground and used it only when necessary. I had set this goal in preparation for my return to school. I was scheduled to begin my graduate studies in psychology in the spring. Getting around campus would be a lot easier if a cane didn't encumber my only usable hand.

Getting to the point where I could walk without a cane reinforced the idea that I could achieve anything if I set my mind to it—including regaining the use of my arm, even though the doctors said the chance of this was increasingly remote. Even in the midst of the never-ending challenges I faced alone on a daily basis, I remained focused on a full recovery. If I could swim using only one arm and leg, the possibilities were indeed limitless.

I also had a lot more energy in the months following the

transplant. I wondered if it was a manifestation of my anger. It was, after all, an anger that could not be directed at anyone or anything. Perhaps fueled by this anger, I also became very confrontational since confrontation was all about acknowledging and therefore speaking the truth. In short, there wasn't room for anything less.

Once, when I was assigned a new primary care physician due to a change in my insurance carrier, I contacted him by phone to renew my prescription for physical therapy and extend the number of sessions.

"Well, it's been over six months since your stroke, so why would you need more physical therapy?" the physician asked. I was fully aware of the anger that rose up within me as I began. "You know, doctor, I'm tired of this *attitude* you physicians have about strokes, because you don't know anything about it. And you do not know anything about *me*."

My voice quivered as I tightened my grip on the phone. At that moment, I was tired of hearing that I had no hope of recovery. In the past, I hadn't responded when doctors made statements like this because I'd simply been too physically weak to address them. Yet as I responded to the physician that day, I knew I had to maintain some semblance of emotional control to be heard. I paused and took a breath, mindful of how I might come across. I spoke calmly and assertively and said, "There are two things you should know about me. I am only twenty-six and I've just had a bone marrow transplant—so I'm going to need a little more time to recover." I paused. "Instead of emphasizing this time constraint, doctor, perhaps, you could encourage patients to give it their all, to not give up hope. There are many who would take what you are saying as the only truth."

My willingness to stand up for myself paid off. The physician calmly replied, "You know, with that attitude, you probably *will* regain use of your arm and leg." He agreed to provide me with a prescription for additional physical therapy, just as I'd requested.

With all the challenges I faced, it was no wonder there were moments when I questioned why I had survived. Death would certainly have been much easier than having to adapt to this new life. It would have been over in an instant, and I would have been forever remembered as a young woman who had been so unfairly taken at the prime of her life. But there was no such ending to my story.

After winning the prescription renewal battle, I was sitting in the rehab waiting room one afternoon when the woman who sat across from me struck up a conversation. "My brother had knee surgery, so I drive him here for his physical therapy appointments," she said. "How about you? Why are you here?"

It was just the two of us in the otherwise empty waiting room. As we chatted, she tried her best to avert her eyes from my left arm and hand, which were, as always, pressed tightly against my chest. Despite her efforts, her eyes honed in on them.

"Oh, I had a stroke several months ago."

"Really? Why did you have a stroke? Was it an aneurysm?" This type of inquiry from strangers was the kind that many members in my support group didn't appreciate because they felt it was simply nobody's business. But I didn't mind the questions at all. In fact, I preferred their curiosity to the alternative: not acknowledging the obvious in any way.

"It was a result of leukemia," I replied.

What followed was the standard response I often received. The young woman's mouth dropped open. Her head then tilted slightly to one side and she scrunched her eyebrows together as the corners of her mouth turned downward. She said, in a high-pitched voice, "Hmm. I'm so sorry." Her statement was followed by an all-too-familiar look, as though she had come across an injured puppy.

People responded to my revelation in one of two ways. One group acknowledged my condition by saying something along the lines of, "I'm so sorry for all you've been through." Framed in exquisite subtlety, their words conveyed an understanding and a sense of compassion—a kinship of sorts. The people in this group knew that suffering can be a part of *every* life.

The other group consisted of those who believed they were somehow above it all, as though they were part of a "privileged few" who had a guarantee that no harm would ever come to them or their loved ones, creating a safe distance between us. This act of distancing conveyed pity and only compounded the disconnect I felt with others, which further heightened my sense that I no longer belonged or fit in.

There were also other reminders that I no longer fit in a world of the able-bodied. There was a daily reminder in the lobby of my building. While waiting for the elevator after my walks or when returning from medical appointments, I'd glance at the door to the stairwell. Less than a year earlier, I'd always had the option of running up the two flights of stairs to the apartment. This was no longer the case.

There were reminders outside of the building, too. A few months after my release from the hospital, Ali and I once went for a drive in San Francisco. Because of my physical limitations, taking long drives became a favorite pastime for us. We ventured first to Union Square, where shoppers scurried about. A sadness came over me because I couldn't imagine a day when I would be able to walk among them, unassisted.

Later, while at Ocean Beach, I recalled how Ali and I used

to walk hand-in-hand along the shore. We could no longer do this because my foot would flop to its side on the unstable sand. Instead, we stood in the paved parking area and observed the beachgoers below. Later, we drove through the Twin Peaks neighborhood and turned the corner to the Castro, one of the United States' first gay neighborhoods. I looked up at the landmark rainbow flag that fluttered above. As we slowly drove in the afternoon traffic, I was struck by how quiet the street was. There was no blaring sound of house music from the bars that had, in the past, seemed to be open at all hours of the day. Also missing were the strapping men—dressed in their customary Levi's and muscle T-shirts—who would spill out of the packed bars and onto the sidewalk, swaying to the music.

"Everything looks so different," I muttered. My voice was so quiet that I doubt Ali heard me.

A few pedestrians walked with canes while others were so rail-thin that their bulky jackets couldn't hide their emaciated states. While we were stopped at a traffic light, a young man in the crosswalk ahead looked right at me and our eyes instantly locked, just as I had locked eyes with Steven in the cancer center lobby. Although it was only a quick glance, I was drawn in. His blank, unfocused gaze seemed familiar somehow.

Suddenly, I had a flashback to my childhood when I was about eight years old. In the early seventies, while Papa was recovering at Guam's Naval Hospital, my siblings and I would come across young men in the corridors and waiting rooms. The soldiers from the Vietnam War were boys, really. I found it odd that although they were in the hospital, they were not dressed like patients. Instead, they wore T-shirts, camouflage pants, and boots. What's more, many did not have visible wounds. However, their eyes—glazed and unblinking—told another story, as though they were lost in another world.

"Everything looks so different," I muttered again, gazing around the streets at men who shared this shell-shocked look.

The Castro felt like a war zone that day, and the young men of my generation were in the midst of a battle. The AIDS epidemic had begun less than a decade before, but in those short years, it had transformed the city. At that time, there was no stopping the disease. Men in their prime, and others, were dying every day.

Why didn't I notice all of this before, I wondered as I looked around. Had I simply turned away when it became too uncomfortable to see what was happening, which was my usual way of dealing with unpleasant truths? How could it be that these men looked the way I felt? How could it be that I suddenly fit in? And how could it be that the city suddenly reflected my own experience?

I sighed. "Everything looks so different."

CHAPTER TWENTY-TWO

Nothing Has Changed

When I first received my diagnosis, Ali had clung to me and proclaimed that nothing had changed. But how could he say that? Everything in my life was so blatantly different than it had been, and I wanted everyone to acknowledge it, no matter what the cost. This was a result of having experienced a catastrophic illness. I had, after all, just dealt with the hardest truth there is: my mortality. If I could confront death, then I could face anything head-on. It compelled me to speak, or at least to recognize the truth.

Ali's words in my hospital room that morning had struck like a heavy blow. I felt that everything *had* changed, including his feelings for me. His words triggered a part of me that had perhaps lain dormant until then, giving me an overwhelming sense that our relationship was doomed.

I was confused by my reaction, by my sudden need to face the truth, so I held in my emotions as he said the words. I didn't understand what I was feeling, and I also knew that I wasn't ready to lose him—not then, at least. In that moment, I could only tuck away the knowledge that I had changed. I had to focus on more important matters—my treatment.

The human spirit seems to find a way of surviving, and early in my hospitalization, I discovered what worked for me. I sensed that for the time being, my survival depended on doing absolutely nothing about my relationship. Instead, I had to focus my energies on getting well. The irony of my situation was that if I were lucky enough to survive, there would later be plenty of time for losing Ali. I instinctively began to say my goodbyes, letting go of him—of "us"—in a number of small ways. I began by focusing, for instance, on our moments together. Once, Ali sat by my hospital bed and held my hand. "You should be at your physical therapy until 11:00, so I'll head out now and run some errands. I'll buy that George Winston cassette you wanted. Okay?"

"Sounds good," I responded. I took a deep breath and thought, *No matter what happens, I'm going to remember this moment and how much I know he loves me.* I stared at our intertwined fingers, which locked our hands together as though they were one. I acted without thought, from that place within that knew all I could do was appreciate our moments together.

Yet there were times when I found it difficult to contain my ever-growing need to speak out about what was, to me, the obvious. Once, in the midst of saying our goodbyes, I impulsively raised the subject of what would become of us. Maybe it was too soon to have that conversation, but at that moment I needed to hear Ali say that he was with me because he wanted to be and not because he felt obligated to be.

"If you want to leave now, you can," I said. "I'll understand." I was astonished by the sound of my own voice—it was flat, as if I were reading aloud something I hadn't written. This statement didn't come from a place of deep feeling; I simply said what had been on my mind all along. If I had allowed myself to feel the emotions I'd buried, I would have instead spoken of my terror at the thought of losing him. Or I would have said that he was truly the one good thing left in my life.

Although I knew it was a risk to raise the subject, I took the chance anyhow, mindful that I needed to accept the outcome.

When did I ever find knowing the truth to be more bearable than not knowing?

Ali's reply was gruff. "What are you talking about? You really think I'm going to just walk away because things are tough right now? I'm not the kind of person who leaves just like that."

I breathed a sigh of relief. I had done what I needed to do for the time being, which meant I could temporarily put the matter to rest.

Shortly before my final release from the hospital, Daddy and I had our first real father-daughter chat. It was difficult to see his face as we spoke since he stood by the window and the morning light poured into the room from behind him. He began by telling me that I had been fortunate to receive such excellent medical care. He reminded me that my chances of surviving leukemia would have been far less if I'd been diagnosed only a few years earlier. He then spoke of how fortunate I was to receive my care from a warm and devoted team of individuals.

"When you're better, you should really think about writing a letter to one of the newspapers," he urged. "Tell them about the people here. I think that would be really good." Daddy paused as he approached my bed. His face and shoulders dropped as if he were preparing himself to bring up a rather difficult matter, perhaps what had been foremost on his mind all along. "You know," he said, "the one thing I am sure of after everything that's happened is how much Ali really loves you. Never forget that. Never. Until now, I never knew just how much he loves you." Daddy's voice trailed off as he brushed tears from his face with the palm of his hand.

"I know, I know," was all I could say. Ali had always been there for me. He was at my bedside night after night, keeping me company until I fell asleep before retiring to his own futon on the waiting room floor. He was there to hold me whenever I became sick from the treatments, wiping the tears from my eyes and reminding me that I would soon be home and "all of this" would soon be over. And he was there, standing beside my bed in our stolen moments alone throughout the day, gently brushing my cheek, saying how much he loved me.

After all of this, how could I ever question Ali's devotion to me? Indeed, he loved me, but we weren't in the real world yet—a place where I sensed his love would be put to the ultimate test.

As I settled into my new life after the transplant, a shadow followed me: wondering when and how our relationship would end. Day and night, I felt a heavy presence in my heart. Once I was diagnosed, we didn't discuss our upcoming marriage nearly as often as we had. In fact, it became a rare topic and a silence grew between us. Ali had said, "We'll just postpone the wedding until you're better." Worse still, we seemed to have different ideas about what "getting better" meant. At some point, the issue of my arm became the telltale sign of our prospects, in his eyes at least. As Ali once pointedly remarked, "When your arm returns, we'll get married." We both looked away from one another at that moment—he looked down at the floor while I glanced out the window.

His words enraged me. Was our future together now contingent on whether I would fully recover? As trite as it sounds, I wanted the person I was planning to spend the rest of my life with to love me for who I was, not for who I used to be or for who he wanted me to be. My eyes widened as I quickly replied. "But, Ali, what if it doesn't return?"

He seemed to be taken aback by my question, as though the thought had never crossed his mind. "Don't ever say that," he said. "I don't want you to ever give up like that."

But I wasn't giving up. I had merely reached a point where I felt that I was moving on. Where was that thin line between acceptance and surrender? For me, accepting my situation meant living my life and acknowledging my limitations at that moment while persisting in my endeavors to regain whatever abilities I could. I refused to put anything "on hold" because of my new circumstances, but he didn't feel the same way. So while he settled comfortably in the realm of "not knowing," I dealt with life's uncertainties by taking great lengths to control whatever I could.

And yet he also did extraordinary things that redeemed his insensitive remarks and that only left me (and him, I suppose) feeling more confused. One of the nicest gestures he or anyone ever made was when he confessed, "You know, I've wanted to understand what it's really like for you, so today I went around doing everything using only one hand. And I tell you, it was hard! I honestly don't know how you do it." This seemingly simple act not only acknowledged my loss but also confirmed that some part of him was trying to accept and understand my predicament.

Late one night, after attending a wedding reception at the St. Francis Hotel in the city, Ali and I joined two other couples who were also on their way home. As the others walked ahead of us, I said, "Ali, can you get the car? It's late and I'm going to have a hard time walking out in the cold." I felt this was a reasonable request, particularly since this was the first occasion on which I'd worn regular shoes without my full leg brace.

"No," Ali sternly replied, almost in a whisper. He didn't look at me. "You're going to walk out with me, like everyone else." I was taken aback by his words. What happened to the once-gentle and considerate man I had known? The one who always ensured that I was comfortable?

Stunned, I asked, "What do you mean? I really think it's best if you get the car. You know how my body stiffens when I'm cold."

"No. You're going to walk out with me," he replied as he continued to look straight ahead.

When we finally reached the others, the women were sitting in the lobby chairs.

"What are you guys doing?" Ali asked. "Aren't you leaving?"

One of the men replied, "We're going to get the car. They're going to wait here. You know, it's the high heels."

Still without looking at me, Ali immediately let go of my hand and walked out the door with the other men. I sensed he understood that he was being unreasonable, and I remained shocked by the way he had spoken to me.

On our drive home, I confronted him about what had just happened. "Don't ever speak to me in that tone of voice again. What was that all about, anyway? Those women have the right not to walk to the car because of their high heels, and I don't for *my* reasons?"

As always, Ali did not respond but was silent and continued to look straight ahead. He seemed to be as confused as I was by what had just occurred. I once read that major life crises can tear apart even the best of relationships. I suppose this is because crisis heightens existing stress. Given our lack of communication, in particular, I felt the chances were next to none that my relationship with Ali could survive a crisis of this magnitude. We shared little of our feelings about my illness and recovery; even today, I cannot say what it was that he went through. I can only speak of my desperate attempts to make sense of things and acknowledge that I may have frequently taken his words and fitted them into what I saw as the problem.

The problem was not whether he loved me. I knew he did. The question had evolved into *how much* he loved me. Did he love me enough to remain in our relationship wholeheartedly, despite the change in our circumstances? It wasn't in his nature to walk out over such things, and I worried that he stayed with me just to do the right thing. If that was the case, it meant that our relationship had become a lie—something I did not want to be a part of.

But, as I had always known, I could still use my remaining time with him to prepare for what I believed would be a period of great sorrow when the relationship ended, perhaps sorrow unlike any other I had known. For the time being, preparing meant staying on course, which entailed listening to my instincts. It also meant continuing, for instance, to appreciate our moments together and firmly believing that doing so would make losing him more bearable.

My experience was perhaps similar to what those who are in mourning go through. They say the grieving process is less complicated (albeit still painful) if there has been time to say goodbye. Something wonderful seems to happen when you're aware that you have finite time with another human being. Moments together are not wasted on trivialities. Instead, being fully present for each moment causes you to cherish your time, which somehow makes letting go much easier in the end. This was the one thing I had: I could say my goodbyes to Ali without later looking back in regret.

My instincts also led me to ignore the callous remarks he unwittingly made from time to time, such as his directive after the wedding: "You're going to walk out with me, like everyone else." It was as if I would hear the comments and then tuck them away in a place that only strengthened my resolve. Outwardly, my response was cold silence. After he'd ask me what was wrong, I'd reply, "Nothing." This only contributed to the ever-growing distance between us. And, as I'd later learn, this way of ignoring things can create a wellspring of anger. When left to fester inside of us, anger becomes blind rage when it is eventually expressed. When the time came for Ali and me to finally discuss things, my rage about the bleak prospects of our relationship was in full force, along with my rage for everything else that had happened.

"What do you want?" I screamed. We'd been out enjoying the day when Ali had again inadvertently made a comment that I deemed inappropriate, thus spurring an all-out battle. As I remember it, he was telling me about progress on the home he had begun building for us to live in after our marriage. In passing, he had referred to it as "my house." This set me off because he had always called it "our house" before I fell ill. It was becoming increasingly difficult to overlook such thoughtless yet telling remarks. He promptly pulled the car onto the side of the road, to a spot overlooking the bay, so we could talk. It was early dusk and the Bay Bridge stood out against the backdrop of San Francisco.

"Tell me what it is that you want!" I cried.

"I don't know," he muttered. "I don't know." His eyes darted from side to side and the furrows on his face deepened. He was clearly struggling to come up with an answer for me— or perhaps for himself. He avoided my eyes altogether and instead looked out toward the bay. Again, he murmured, "I don't know."

As always, his apparent confusion only intensified my anger. How could he sit there so calmly? Why wasn't he strong enough to fight for us?

"Then why don't you just say it, Ali? Say it, damn it! Tell me what we both know!" I cried. By this time, I was so enraged that I wasn't even aware of what I was asking of him. I seemed to be operating on a level where the words simply came out of my mouth without having any clue of where they were heading. But I stayed with it and trusted my instincts. "I want to hear you say what we both know!"

"Say wh-what?" He was at a loss. In my desperation to understand him, I, too, became quickly confused by what was happening. All possible explanations for his behavior came to mind. Was he truly as lost as he appeared to be regarding the matter? Or, did he simply lack the courage to do what he knew he had to do? After all, if he were to walk out on me, he would forever be branded as the bad guy. I wondered if, on a deeper level, some part of him was forcing me to end the relationship because he was too afraid to do it himself.

He had said "my house," not "our house." Was that his way of passively telling me (and possibly himself) that the relationship was over? Even though I knew it would be devastating to lose him, I would have had more respect for him if he had been honest and forthright about his intentions rather than leaving us in the state where we found ourselves—one of prolonged uncertainty.

Suddenly, everything became clear to me and I knew what I needed to hear. There was no reason for him to mince words. Slamming my hand on the dashboard, I yelled, "I want to hear you say that you don't want to be with me because I can't have children. Say it, damn it! Why can't you just say it?" There it was once again: my compelling need for the truth.

"No," he whispered as he shook his head and his eyes welled with tears.

"No, it isn't even that anymore. It—it was when they rushed into your hospital room that one morning. I thought you were going to die. I was *so* scared. I was standing behind the round window watching and thinking, 'Oh shit, I'm gonna lose her.' It scared me so much that I can't explain what happened to me because *I* don't even understand it. I think to myself, okay, I can accept that we won't have children, but then you'll die and I'll be alone. I know it doesn't make any sense, but that's what I'm afraid of."

For the first time since this had all begun, I felt compassion for Ali. What had my illness done to him? His position of having alternatives—staying and dealing with what had happened or leaving for a fresh start with someone else—didn't seem appealing. In fact, it appeared to be the very source of his quandary. No matter what he decided, he would be haunted by "what ifs." He would always want what he didn't have, particularly if he chose to remain with me. The one thing I was certain of was that a life without him would be far better than living with him in misery. And so my compassion for him was fleeting. As always, my rage took over—and rightly so since he had just answered the question that had been in the back of my mind all along. Although it wasn't because I was unable to have children, his answer was still a resounding "No." No, he didn't love me enough to see this through.

While I may have been ready to hear the truth, I wasn't yet fully prepared to face it head-on. Not surprisingly, my next move was to pull away from this highly emotional and, quite frankly, scary exchange.

"Is there anyone out there who can guarantee they won't die on you?" I asked, taking us away from a place of feeling to one that was more rational. Although my voice had lowered, I still spoke through clenched teeth.

"No. It's only with you that I feel this way," Ali answered. "Like I said, this doesn't make any sense. I sometimes feel God has been giving us signs that we shouldn't be together. Like your being sick so soon before the wedding, then losing the ring. Maybe they're signs."

Losing the ring. I had been hoping to forget about that.

Ali's mother had purchased what was to be my wedding ring during her annual visit to Iran, but it had been confiscated by customs officials when she tried to bring it to the United States in the midst of my illness. After hearing the news, I felt—for one small moment—the way that Ali did. *Perhaps it's a sign,* I'd thought. It wasn't long, though, before I found myself dismissing the event as a meaningless coincidence, something I rarely did. I suppose it had been my way of believing that we at least had some control over our own destinies, thus not leaving things solely to fate—for fate was clearly not on our side.

"You sound like an old lady, for Christ's sake," I sneered, mocking Ali's confession. "So, it happened. Maybe it doesn't even mean anything. Why can't we just move on?" Pulling back from my feelings, I was the one who was once again avoiding the issues.

Looking back on it today, I can see we were caught up in a dance of one taking a step back as the other moved forward, all the while remaining at a standstill. The impact that would have occurred if we had both moved forward at the same time probably would have served as a catalyst for action or for confronting the issues.

Although I was unaware of exactly what we were going through at the time, I sensed that we were in the midst of some sort of process—adjustment, perhaps. In her book *On Death and Dying,* psychiatrist Elisabeth Kübler-Ross examines five stages of the dying process: denial, anger, bargaining, depression, and acceptance. Collectively known as the grieving process, these are the very stages Ali and I went through. Perhaps we were grieving for the person I once was or for the life we could have shared. We went through it blindly and, sadly, in isolation.

Would it have been fair for us to deny our own progress through the stages just to keep up with one another? No. Grief is a uniquely individual experience. Frequently faltering between any two stages, it was so draining for me to make sense of my own experience that there simply wasn't enough left over for me to process what Ali was going through. And so, we danced.

"This also happened to me, you know," Ali once professed during our ever-increasing arguments.

"Yeah, but the difference between us is that *you* can walk away without ever having to look back. I can't. Don't you get the difference yet?" While he could later bury the memory of this whole ordeal beneath layers of illusion, I could not. Once he settled into a new life with a wife and children, would he ever want or need to look back at this time? Probably not. It would not be as easy for me, so how dare he compare his experience to mine?

I ended this exchange with one final blow, even harsher than the last. "I've learned one thing from all this, Ali. When the ship sinks, it's every man for himself." The impact of my words was immediate. His eyes filled with tears and he jerked back as if to lessen the blow. As always, my words were brutal and to the point—and more important, they were deliberately meant to tear his heart. It was the only way I could make him feel a little of what I was feeling.

"This," Ali said, "is why I will never love anyone again, because this is what happens—you just get hurt. I'm going to get married without love and have children, and that's it."

"Oh, please. This is how you love someone? By jumping ship?" Again, he had a clear reaction to my jab. We talked past each other, each making a case without stopping to really hear what the other said. It was no surprise that the relationship rapidly deteriorated.

In the end, my decision to leave him seemed impulsive to those around me. After another one of our petty arguments over the telephone, I ended the discussion with something along the lines of "okay, that's it—it's over." I followed the crescendo with a dramatic slam of the receiver. The one thing I knew, above all else, was that I was no longer willing to pretend nothing was wrong. As always, I operated purely on instinct.

There were many times when Ali and I had been close to a breakup during the three years that had passed since my final release from the hospital, so I was somewhat accustomed to feeling devastated. It was different this time, though. I could imagine a life without him and not feel threatened. I suppose the "small steps" that I had taken leading to the breakup had worked after all. There was no turning back for me.

"Are you sure you know what you're doing?" my sisters would ask.

"Yes," I would firmly answer. "It was all a lie anyway."

Perhaps taking it harder than anyone else in my family, my mother cried upon hearing the news. As she hugged me, I sensed two distinct reactions. On the one hand, she was shattered that her Favorite would not be marrying, and on the other hand, I sensed her independent side was proud that I'd had the strength and courage to leave on my own terms. Not surprisingly, I had these two conflicting sides in me as well.

For the next several days, I avoided Ali's phone calls— except for perhaps buying time, talking things over had never worked for us. Later that week, I mailed him a four-page letter in which I emphasized my need to end a situation that I saw as hopeless, telling him that it had only been a matter of time before we parted ways. Writing helped to keep my anger in check, and I liked the fact that I could go at my own pace without getting distracted by what he might or might not say.

"Have a good life," I wrote in closing the letter. The phrase appealed to the part of me—the one underneath all the anger and bitterness—that believed our relationship was ultimately out of our hands so there wasn't anyone to blame. Some things are just not meant to be. This phrase allowed me to let go of him without bitterness, even if it was only for that one small moment.

Many of those around me believed that ending the relationship by completely breaking it off and refusing to speak with him was extreme—they felt he didn't deserve such treatment. During the height of our difficulties, Ali had even once commented, "I know that one day you'll cut me off, just like you've done with some of your friends."

I had developed a solid reputation for what others saw as my curious ability to act as if certain individuals in my life no longer existed. But I had grown tired of this long-held family practice, which I had first observed when my mother feuded with her siblings back in Guam. For years, I wanted to prove to myself that I could somehow overcome it. Surely, there must be more adult ways of handling conflict.

So later, at Ali's urging, we remained in contact for a few months. But I found this approach was simply too painful to bear. No one could ever understand the hurt and humiliation I felt whenever I heard, for example, about the dates his relatives would arrange for him in hopes of finding him a suitable Iranian wife. Was I really expected to just stand aside and graciously take it all in? No. Now more than ever, I sensed that my very survival depended on nothing less than a clean break, for the pain was all too fresh and raw. After months of convincing myself that I was strong and sophisticated enough to maintain a "friendship" with him, I finally broke down.

"Please, Ali," I cried over the telephone. "Just leave me alone to get over this, and you can go your own way. Why do you insist that I be a part of your life when it's so hard for me?" For the first time, I wasn't coming from a place of anger. At my weakest point, all I could do was plead for his help. "Maybe we can be friends, but not now. Not like this. This is too hard."

Ali was quiet and softly muttered, "Okay, okay."

It was the last we spoke. I received a Christmas card from him later that year, and it was as if I was in automatic pilot mode as I took the unopened card and gently placed it in the trash. As I'd always known, there was no turning back for me. Che-Che, who was there at the time, immediately reached for the card and yelled in disbelief, "No. What are you doing? I'm going to open it!"

"NO!" I cried. "There's no point. It's finished." What could a few kind words in a card do except to delay the inevitable ending of our presence in each other's lives?

I instructed my friends and family not to inform me of any news they heard about Ali. Perhaps the one thing that would make me fall apart was hearing he had married and moved on with his life. Someone once said that the length of time to get over a broken relationship is typically half the time the relationship lasted. But getting over him—even if it took years—was inconceivable. I could not imagine a day when I wouldn't miss him.

Yet despite my sorrow, the breakup felt right somehow, as though it was meant to be. This peculiar feeling reminded me of an instance that had occurred years before. Soon after becoming engaged, Ali and I had gone through some old photographs from our early dating years and come across one that he had taken of me standing by a pier in Sausalito. He confessed that shortly thereafter, he brought the photo with him when he visited a psychic whose storefront he passed on his drive home from work each night. Paying attention to a psychic was quite out of character for him, since he wasn't a believer in the metaphysical.

"I was just curious, so I decided to drop by," he explained.

The psychic began by saying that he would be very successful in "something that has to do with homes," as she put it. When he informed me of this incident, Ali had just established himself as a developer, building homes in the South Bay Area, so her words were all the more powerful.

"I then handed her your photo and asked what she could tell me about you," Ali said.

"No," she had firmly stated. "She's not the one you're going to marry."

As he shared this with me, we reveled in the irony of it all since our wedding was only months away.

Ali mentioned one other thing the psychic had said, which at the time made no sense to either of us.

"She's a *very* strong woman."

EPILOGUE

San Francisco Bay Area, November 2010

"My work in patient advocacy began after my own experience with the disease. In 1988, I was diagnosed with acute myelogenous leukemia," I began my presentation. I then paused briefly and quickly gauged the way I was seated on the chair, to help relax my arm and leg that had tensed up. I then continued, "As the American Cancer Society staff representative assigned to work with this hospital, I must say that I feel particularly privileged to be working with your team since I received my treatment at this very facility. As of this year, I am twenty-two years post-bone marrow transplant."

When I finished my introduction, jaws dropped and there were audible gasps, which were followed by an immediate but brief silence that filled the room. I had received the same reaction during talks I had given to the cancer committees at my various assigned facilities over the years. For that one instant, the medical professionals always looked at me as though I were one of them—an equal sitting at the table. But it was also different that night, for I was one of their very own after all: a survivor who had returned from the front lines, perhaps affirming that their work indeed made a difference. As one of the nurses said to me after the meeting, "You should tell everyone you know about your long-term survival. As nurses, we only remember the ones that don't make it, and we rarely

Suzanne—my former nurse—and I meet up at a patient advocacy event held by my non-profit employer. San Francisco 2001.

212 JULIANE CORN LEE

ever again meet the ones who do."

Like the medical team I, too, was making a difference, albeit in my own way, and I was proud of my work. I felt privileged to have my passion also be my life's work. Connecting with other survivors and hearing their stories was particularly inspiring to me, and it made my work even more meaningful and personally enriching. It affirmed that there was a reason for all that I'd endured. Even early on, I knew finding the meaning in my suffering would be an essential part of healing.

As I drove on Ashby Avenue on my way home that evening, I glanced at the hospital's fourth floor and saw the window of what had once been my room. It brought me back to the countless days when I would sit in the orange vinyl armchair and look out towards the busy street below. *If they only knew how lucky they were to simply ride in a car*, I'd reflect. For the first time in over two decades, I understood just how far I had come. That evening was powerful because it made me realize I had come full circle. I felt as though I were home. At that point in my life, regrets were a rarity as I focused instead on my gratitude for having survived as I'd done—and on my undeniable ability to reinvent myself.

While some might deem my circumstances as tragic, I saw my illness as a vital part of my life that contributed to the woman I had become. When the unspeakable happens, it is beyond our control, yet these situations allow us the opportunity to choose what follows. I spoke publicly about cancer education, disability, survivorship, and, of course, the ever-present grief that comes along with survival. In keeping with my mother's tradition of storytelling, I also began writing about my experience, composing at first journal entries that evolved into short essays, and eventually resulting in this book.

In the aftermath I came to find a voice, and it is that voice—that breaking of silence—that has saved me.

Grateful acknowledgment is made to the following for permission to reprint previously published material:

"I Ching: A New Interpretation For Modern Times" by Sam Reifler. Bantam Books, Inc., 1974. Used by permission.

"San Francisco (You've Got Me)" written by J. Morali, H. Belolo, B. Whitehead, P. Hurtt. © Scorpio Music, S.A./Can't Stop Music, 1977. Used by permission.